HOW YOUR TEENAGER IS WIRED

discovering who GOD made

YOUR TEENAGER *to be*

Katie Brazelton

FOREWORD BY DOUG FIELDS

How Your Teenager Is Wired
Discovering Who God Made Your Teenager To Be

Copyright © 2011 Katie Brazelton

group.com
simplyyouthministry.com

Credits
Author: Katie Brazelton
Executive Developer: Nadim Najm
Chief Creative Officer: Joani Schultz
Editor: Rob Cunningham
Cover Art and Production: Jeff Storm, Veronica Lucas, and Riley Hall
Back Cover Author Picture: Images by Dwayne
Production Manager: DeAnne Lear

Unless otherwise indicated, all Scripture quotations are taken from the *Holy Bible*, New Living Translation, copyright © 1996, 2004, 2007. Used by permission of Tyndale House Publishers, Inc., Carol Stream, Illinois 60188. All rights reserved.

Scripture quotations marked The Message are taken from *The Message*. Copyright © 1993, 1994, 1995, 1996, 2000, 2001, 2002. Used by permission of NavPress Publishing Group.

Scripture quotations marked NKJV are taken from the *New King James Version*. Copyright © 1982 by Thomas Nelson, Inc. Used by permission. All rights reserved.

Scripture quotations marked NIV are taken from THE HOLY BIBLE, NEW INTERNATIONAL VERSION®, NIV® Copyright © 1973, 1978, 1984, 2010 by Biblica, Inc.™ Used by permission. All rights reserved worldwide.

Scripture quotations marked TNIV are taken from HOLY BIBLE, TODAY'S NEW INTERNATIONAL VERSION®. Copyright © 2001, 2005 by Biblica®. Used by permission of Biblica®. All rights reserved worldwide.

Library of Congress Cataloging-in-Publication Data
Brazelton, Katie, 1950-
    How your teenager is wired : discovering who God made your teenager to be / Katie Brazelton.
        p. cm.
    ISBN 978-0-7644-4705-1 (pbk.)
    1. Parent and teenager--Religious aspects--Christianity. 2. Child rearing--Religious aspects--Christianity. I. Title.
    BV4529.B694 2011
    248.8'45--dc22
                            2011001076

ISBN 978-0-7644-4705-1

10 9 8 7 6 5 4 3   20 19 18 17 16 15 14

Printed in the United States of America.

The Lord replied to Jeremiah, "Don't say, 'I'm too young,' for you must go wherever I send you and say whatever I tell you."

—Jeremiah 1:7

CONTENTS

FOREWORD
DOUG FIELDS

After more than 30 years in youth ministry, I've figured out a few important lessons:

- I will never regain the "cool" status I held in the eyes of teenagers when I was 21.

- I should delegate all projects requiring technology to younger people.

- Teenage guys can drive all-you-can-eat pizzerias out of business.

More importantly, I've learned that my impact on a teenager's life is nowhere as potent as the impact you can have as a parent. Youth pastors and volunteer youth workers play *important* roles in your teenager's life—but you play the most *vital* and *important* role!

Some people talk about teenagers being the church of tomorrow. I don't believe that! I'm convinced that teenagers who are bold enough to follow Jesus are the church of *today*. They don't have to wait until they're older to do something big for God; they can do it now—and understanding their unique mission is a key step in accomplishing big things for God. And as a parent of three teenagers myself, I know that a parent's gentle tug, inspired motivation, and well-timed words of love and encouragement are so helpful toward a teenager taking a step toward God.

That's why I'm so excited about this book. I've known Katie Brazelton since 1992, and I had the privilege of serving as youth pastor to her son and daughter. She's the real deal! She has sought and discovered God's incredible purpose for her life, and she's turned her passion into her living. For many years now, Katie's primary focus has been to help people discover God's unique mission for their lives. Now she wants to help you help your son/daughter.

This book reflects Katie's passionate commitment to her calling. Her insights will guide you as discover your unique life purpose and will inspire you as you accompany your teenager on that same path.

As a parent, I love seeing my children discover God's mission for their lives, and I value my own unique purpose, too. While working through this book with your teenager, commit to praying for God's leading, take time to ask good questions, and remember to listen and truly hear your child's heart. Every moment you spend helping your child discover their unique purpose will be time well spent.

If you haven't gone through the adventure of finding your unique life purpose, consider meeting with some other adults to discover what God has created each of you to do—even as you walk with your teenager on this journey.

I pray that you and your teenager experience a deeper relationship and incredible discoveries as you pursue God's best for your life!

Doug Fields

INTRODUCTION

When my son and daughter were teenagers in the 1990s, I filled out a fun parental quiz (lightly in pencil) about their likes and dislikes. It asked about their favorite school subject, teacher, and friend, as well as their favorite pet, color, meal, dessert, hobby, car, song, book, movie, and TV show—among a slew of other things. Frankly, I struggled with many of the questions, not having a clue how my kids would answer. Before you conclude that I was a terrible mother, I challenge you to try such a quiz yourself!

The point of the exercise was for parents to open a line of communication with their teenagers by discussing the quiz. As I shared my answers with my kids, we were all shocked to discover that I knew very little about them. My combined score for both of them was a measly 23 percent, and I did a lot of erasing that day—to replace my wrong answers with their correct ones! How could this be? I was a good mom; some even said that I was a great mom. My entire life revolved around my kids. In fact, with my teacher's schedule, I was home when they were home after school, on holidays, and for the entire summer. How could I not know everything about them? What had we been talking about all those years, if not discovering more about one another?

Fast-forward to present day: My two married kids and their families came to visit me in Maui, where I was living for one year to write this book series. Halfway through our time together, I realized that we hadn't talked about anything of substance. Oh, sure, we had discussed dinner plans, kids' naps, the weather, fun outings, snorkeling equipment, the most recent movies we'd seen, or their latest sports injury. And yes, we had snapped tons of pictures, laughed, hugged, explored, shopped, watched hula shows, searched out yogurt shops, and enjoyed sunsets together—but not one word had been uttered about...

- *How's your small group going at church?*

- *Have you made any Christian friends in your new neighborhood?*

- *Are you being a good husband and spiritual leader of your household?*

- *What do you enjoy most about being a wife and mother?*

- *What latest miracle has God performed in your life?*

- *How can I pray for you?*

I was mortified when that realization hit me. How could I be ignoring the really important side of my kids' lives—their *insides*, their heart and soul? It was one level of neglect not to know their favorite song or book, but this was an all-new low for me not to have checked how they were doing in the Lord.

I wish something like this book had been available to me when I was a young married mom; and later a middle-aged, single mom; and now a spry grandmother of two. What a gift it would've been for me if only someone would've reminded me to engage in meaningful conversations with my kids about God's unique plan for their lives, based on how they've been wired. Other than the topic of salvation, is there any more important conversation we can have with our teenagers than the one about their personal surrender to God's will for their life? The bottom line is no. Nothing is more important in our parenting role.

And what a gift it'll be for me in the future to talk with each of my grandchildren about the awesome and bold purpose God has in mind for them.

You're about to embark on a life-changing journey with your teenager. Enjoy it to the hilt! Don't let a decade or two fly by. Now is the time.

Blessings,

Katie Brazelton

PART 1

PREPARING
FOR CHANGE

CHAPTER 1

HOW TO HAVE THE BEST POSSIBLE PARENT-TEENAGER RELATIONSHIP

For the Lord is the one who shaped the mountains, stirs up the winds, and reveals his thoughts to mankind. He turns the light of dawn into darkness and treads on the heights of the earth. The Lord God of Heaven's Armies is his name! (Amos 4:13).

Life purpose is a never-ending cry of the human heart. Our teenagers' minds are filled with questions:

- *Why was I born?*

- *Where do I fit in this world?*

- *What does God want me to do after high school?*

- *What major should I declare in college?*

- *What should I be when I grow up?*

- *Will my dreams ever come true?*

- *Is this all there is to life?*

- *What on earth am I here for?*

In response to this cry, parents pray for some process or some person to come along to encourage their teenagers to lead more abundantly blessed lives of purpose and significance—to live the lives they were meant to live. They want their children to know Christ as their Savior and to be joyful, peaceful, holy, healthy, wise, and fulfilled doing God's will. They want them to have a rewarding vocation and career in or outside their home—and to become independent and self-sufficient.

Don't parents dream that their teenagers will discover how they've been wired with unique, God-given giftedness? That they'll understand who they were made to be and how they've been readied to answer God's call on their life? That they'll launch successfully into God's distinct plan?

Well, don't worry about trying to do all that ultra-parenting alone. You have the right resource in your hand. Let's get your teenager raised—on purpose, with a passionate purpose. Your reward for lovingly serving your young adult in this way will be a relational bond like none other.

As we begin, it's important to point out that you'll have the unparalleled privilege of discussing God's three purposes for your teenager's life. And it's most effective to do this in true *trifecta* fashion—with all three purposes working together in perfect harmony to unleash God's best!

Biblical Purpose Trifecta: 1-2-3

1. Universal Purpose: Love God by belonging to Christ.

Your purpose is to love God by choosing to be transformed into a new person in the image of Christ. This happens by reading God's Word and allowing the Holy Spirit to teach you to surrender to Jesus Christ as Lord. This means that, with the help of your church family (including prayer partners, accountability partners, and mentors), you're committed to a life of holiness, integrity, right motives, peace, and worshipping your Creator—and helping others to do the same.

Scriptural Basis

- *Jesus replied, "'You must love the Lord your God with all your heart, all your soul, and all your mind.' This is the first and greatest commandment" (Matthew 22:37-38).*

- *Don't copy the behavior and customs of this world, but let God transform you into a new person by changing the way you think. Then you will learn to know God's will for you, which is good and pleasing and perfect (Romans 12:2).*

- *Jesus told him, "I am the way, the truth, and the life. No one can come to the Father except through me" (John 14:6).*

2. Universal Purpose: Love God by loving others.

Your purpose is to love God by doing today—with love—what matters today in the responsibilities, daily tasks, and major roles God has assigned you. This includes honoring your Maker by serving with Christ-like love in all your life domains: personal, family, relationships, school, job, ministry, and community. This means that you trust in the Lord for strength and power to fulfill your commitments and meet the challenges that drive your day at home, school, work, and church, and in your neighborhood and ministry setting, and on your mission field.

Scriptural Basis

- Jesus added, *"A second [commandment] is equally important: 'Love your neighbor as yourself'" (Matthew 22:39).*

- *This is the message you have heard from the beginning: We should love one another (1 John 3:11).*

- *No one has ever seen God. But if we love each other, God lives in us, and his love is brought to full expression in us (1 John 4:12).*

3. Unique Purpose: Glorify God by fulfilling your "This I Must Do" Dream.

Your purpose is to glorify God by doing the "One Big Thing" God commissioned you—and you alone—to do to help build the kingdom. This unique, individual, significant purpose directs you to pursue your God-designed life mission with pure joy and to deliver your God-inspired life message to those you're eager to serve. This purpose is God's personalized gift to you, and it's a dream that reflects your passionate ache, your Divine Urge, your heart's desire, and the fascination that was planted in your soul before you were even born. It's what drives your life—what you feel you must do. It's what you're called to do—what you feel you *can't not do*! But you must decide if you'll actually take on this huge commitment to make this eternal contribution that's obviously impossible to do without God's help.

Scriptural Basis

- *"I [Jesus] brought glory to you here on earth by completing the work you gave me to do" (John 17:4).*

- *"In the same way that you gave me [Jesus] a mission in the world, I give them a mission in the world" (John 17:18 The Message).*

- *Take delight in the Lord, and he will give you your heart's desires (Psalm 37:4).*

This third purpose—an individual's unique, "This I Must Do" dream—is the focus of this book.

Fulfill Your God-Given, "This I Must Do" Dream

God is famous for planting *must-do* assignments in people's hearts. Consider these life-changing ones:

- **Noah,** build an ark before the great flood. (Genesis 6:13-21)

- **Abram,** go to the land I'll show you—without knowing any specifics. (Genesis 12:1-3)

- **Sarah,** you'll be the mother of nations at the age of 90. (Genesis 17:15-16)

- **Moses,** go to Pharaoh and demand the release of my people. (Exodus 3:10, 20)

- **Gideon,** go with the strength you have and rescue Israel from the Midianites. (Judges 6:12-16)

- **Samuel,** anoint David king (in spite of ensuing turmoil). (1 Samuel 16:12-13)

- **John the Baptist,** prepare the way for me. (Luke 1:13-17)

- **Mary,** you're a virgin but you'll give birth to a Son who will reign with an everlasting kingdom. (Luke 1:28-38)

- **Peter,** feed my lambs. (John 21:15-17)

- **Paul,** proclaim the good news to the Gentiles. (Galatians 1:13-16)

The list goes on and on—moments when God commissions ordinary people to do extraordinary things that take a lifetime to see to final completion or when God calls ordinary people to complete an impossible task that defines and shapes the rest of their lives. Why would you or your teenager be an exception to that pattern of the ordinary person being used to do the extraordinary? God is glorified when we're stretched beyond our personal ability to complete an impossible task.

What about God's call on your life?

So, you want your teenager to answer God's call and travel boldly down the pathway to purpose, but have you lost sight of your own big dreams, secret hopes, and deepest longings? You want to bring more glory to God with your life, but are you carrying such heavy weights of exhaustion, fear, doubt, regrets, hopelessness, boredom, loneliness, or sin that you've forgotten how to sing, play, laugh, and pray to unleash your own creativity and dreams—let alone help your teenager do so? An underlying premise of this book is that you can't expect to help your teenager discover and fulfill God's all-encompassing, best plan if you yourself haven't given serious thought to your own purpose for the second half of your life—AK (After Kids) and WG (While Grandparenting).

Worshipping God through parenting

You may say, "I worship God with my life by being a great parent!" I couldn't agree more that parenting is an incredible way to worship and bring glory to God. I was a single mom for most of my kids' lives (after my young husband had two heart attacks/surgeries, left our marriage as he struggled with a fear of dying, and then died soon after) so I know it's a huge job to parent. In fact, I know it's one of God's most precious ordinations into ministry—the ministry of parenting. We certainly have to be called and blessed to walk that walk with grace.

As children and teenagers begin to learn to love others, share Jesus, connect with people, grow in their faith, serve others, and worship God, somebody must model those universal life-purpose principles for them and love them unconditionally when they fall short. They can't just raise themselves into Christ-likeness. And in the meantime, they have constant human needs for food, shelter, and clothing—and also human desires for safety, security, love, belonging, happiness, self-esteem, respect, and creativity. The job and joy of a parent is to raise God's kids, who are simply on loan to us! And we're to be the wind beneath their wings as they learn to soar into the lifetime dream God has reserved for them.

Some BIG dreams are common to many

Allow me to clarify something. Certain *big* dreams are common to many people. For example, God gives some generalized lifetime dreams that revolve around spiritual growth, life roles, and seasonal purposes:

- Worship God and serve in fellowship with others who love Jesus

- Be accountable to a few spiritually mature friends who help me grow in my faith

- Get a good education that allows me to work in my area of God-given passion

- Be happily married to a faithful, Christ-following spouse

- Raise healthy, kind, and smart children who love Jesus

- Bless my family with financial security, a safe environment, and great memories

- Be lovingly available to my grandchildren and aging parents

I'm the first to applaud each of these dreams, goals, and purposes as being richly significant. They certainly cause countless people to lead fruitful and blessed lives. Because these big dreams are common to so many people, they're listed at this point to acknowledge the importance of them as assignments from God. These mutual dreams won't be the focus of this book, though, because they're not exclusive to one person; they're an incredible blessing for many Christ-followers.

Interestingly, the Bible is clear that we all have specific, unique, broad-reaching, kingdom-building work to do that was entrusted to us alone. That work is different from our intense seasonal roles, such as parenting or grandparenting. If our life mission were limited to parenting only, for example, notice how the meaning of these two verses would narrow tremendously:

For we are God's masterpiece. He has created us anew in Christ Jesus, so we can do the good things he planned for us long ago [**in our own households**] *(Ephesians 2:10).*

Don't act thoughtlessly, but understand what the Lord wants you to do [**as a good parent to your children**] *(Ephesians 5:17).*

God didn't tell us to continue to limit our lifetime dream, our role in this world, our mission on earth to only our own families, even after our children are adults. Our parenting days are not only a gift to us, but they're also a boot camp and a serious training ground for us to have more influence in a wider arena later on.

Your unique purpose...beyond parenting

Let's turn our focus to your most far-reaching, lifetime dream. Perhaps you've been able to pursue this dream as you've been parenting your children, but I know that many adults discover or rediscover that dream as parenting days wind to a close. It's OK to admit that you, a fabulously wonderful parent, may be asking God these questions:

- What about me? I love my children, but I also long to make a difference in the world. You gave me this passionate ache in my heart.

- My teenagers won't always be at home. What purpose will I have after they're raised? I'd love to rediscover the fascination in my soul that you orchestrated specifically for me!

- When I was young, I felt like you'd given me such lofty dreams, in addition to parenting. What happened to my other Divine Urge?

We're God's Ambassador to the World

Our "This I Must Do" mission is to tell others about Jesus in the individualized way God designed us to do it! Just for fun, try to insert into these passages a limiting parental phrase like these: *within your family, in my household,* or *as a good parent to my children.*

- **Isaiah's Answer to God's Call.** *Then I heard the Lord asking, "Whom should I send as a messenger to this people? Who will go for us?" I [Isaiah] said, "Here I am. Send me" (Isaiah 6:8).*

- **Produce Lasting Fruit.** *"You didn't choose me. I [Jesus] chose you. I appointed you to go and produce lasting fruit, so that the Father will give you whatever you ask for, using my name" (John 15:16).*

- **I'm Bound by the Spirit to Go.** *"But my life is worth nothing to me unless I use it for finishing the work assigned me by the Lord Jesus— the work of telling others the Good News about the wonderful grace of God" (Acts 20:24).*

- **God Equips Christians With Spiritual Gifts.** *In his grace, God has given us different gifts for doing certain things well (Romans 12:6).*

- **Christ's Representatives.** *And God has given us this task of reconciling people to him (2 Corinthians 5:18).*

- **God's Mighty Power.** *Now all glory to God, who is able, through his mighty power at work within us, to accomplish infinitely more than we might ask or think (Ephesians 3:20).*

- **Encouragement for Christians.** *So we keep on praying for you, asking our God to enable you to live a life worthy of his call. May he give you the power to accomplish all the good things your faith prompts you to do (2 Thessalonians 1:11).*

- **Offer Your Life to God.** *But you should keep a clear mind in every situation. Don't be afraid of suffering for the Lord. Work at telling others the Good News, and fully carry out the ministry God has given you (2 Timothy 4:5).*

- **Paul's Assignment.** *I [Paul] have been sent to proclaim faith to those God has chosen and to teach them to know the truth that shows them how to live godly lives....It is by the command of God our Savior that I have been entrusted with this work for him (Titus 1:1, 3).*

- I'm so exhausted from raising my children. Will you ever renew my passion for the burden you placed on my heart for the world?

- Being a parent is a privilege; in fact, it's one of the finest gifts you've ever given me. But what about the other distinct life mission you gave me that will allow me to make a significant contribution to the kingdom-at-large?

God speaks. We listen.

The Bible tells us in Amos 4:13 that the Lord God Almighty reveals his thoughts to mankind. Yes, it really does say that we can expect to hear, see, or somehow understand God's thoughts. Scripture tells us to expect revelation!

And by the way, it's natural to have a strange reaction to the hard-to-comprehend idea that you've got a fascinating, custom-made purpose assigned by God. For example, you may feel…

- "I'm not worthy enough, smart enough, or holy enough to shoulder the responsibility of a personalized, impassioned life mission that God will reveal to me—besides parenting."

- "The dream I'm sensing must be of my own making because of prideful and selfish desires I have—and besides, I really need to stay focused on my family."

- "God, you're a taskmaster, and I know you'll assign me something too difficult and too unappealing—and I won't want to do it, after I finish raising my children. Frankly, I don't really want to know what my mission is, because I don't want to end up as an overseas missionary."

- "I don't have the right motives, spiritual gifts, or character traits to complete the new task—and, anyway, I'm comfortable in the current role you delegated to me. I love being a spouse and parent!"

The list of reactions to God's call is endless. The truth is that none of us is good enough to measure up to the precious task of parenting or of doing something else equally magnificent for God beyond parenting. And we all have tons of doubts, concerns, and fears. Fortunately, it's only by the grace and power of God that we'll be able to answer the long-term call on our lives so we can't ever boast that it's of our own doing.

Just like Moses, who begged God in Exodus 4 to send someone else to talk to Pharaoh, you may be praying at this point that God would please take back your revealed life purpose. Have you ever wished that you could hide in your comfort zone as a parent by leaving your apron strings tied to your teenager a tad bit longer?

Please hear my heart on this, when I urge you to move the focus off yourself and onto a passionate God, who has entrusted you with purpose-filled daydreams and elaborate imaginings, most probably for your post-child-rearing days. God has designed a perfect "second-half-of-life" purpose for you, and God wants you to prepare yourself now to follow hard after your vision to further the kingdom. And if you've already been pursuing God's wonderfully unique purpose for you, your influence and impact can grow as your teenagers enter their young adult years.

I wish that someone had written words of encouragement like this for me when I was a young mom! It would've saved me years of tears, wrong turns, and frustrations by helping me be calm and God-confident enough to capture an inkling of the lifetime dream that God had laid out for me—in its own season. I wish I had known that God had reserved a "This I Must Do" purpose for me to enjoy when the timing was right—one that would cause me to become more like Jesus Christ. But I didn't sit still long enough to know that I'd been called to...

- humbly serve those who were seeking their life purpose

- unleash my passion for discipling others

- lean into my spiritual gifts of teaching, encouragement, and leadership

And what about all the other insights I might have learned about my motives, relationships, values, opportunities, and other great stuff? I could've gotten a decade-long jump on living out the passion-mission-vision that God orchestrated solely for me, after my kids were grown, married, and transferred out-of-state by their employers—without my consent!

True, even if I had received a monumental vision from God…

- sin would've still blocked me time and time again from moving forward

- circumstances would've still thrown up roadblocks every time I turned around

- my own doubts and fears would've still sabotaged my progress

- people would've still disappointed me over and over again in ministry

But you know what? I would have…

- learned sooner about the importance of trusting and obeying God

- caused less harm to others, because I'd have been focused on the truth and goodness and significance assigned to my life—as a parent and also as an ambassador for God to the world

- experienced joy in knowing that my life mattered in the greater design of God's plan—even after parenting

Keep that background in mind—you have a distinct, passionate, individualized purpose on earth (beyond those holy, irreplaceable, significance-filled purposes common to many, like parenting). It's time to dig in. In the next chapter, I'll give you our plan of attack—how you're going to help your teenager discover how he or she has been wired by God to fulfill a unique life purpose—after you, first, put on your own life mission oxygen mask. Bottom line, you are being asked to invite God to reveal your own "This I Must Do" purpose, too!

CHAPTER 2

HOW TO GET THE MOST FROM THIS BOOK

Two people are better off than one, for they can help each other succeed. If one person falls, the other can reach out and help. But someone who falls alone is in real trouble (Ecclesiastes 4:9-10).

So far, we've established four truths about parenting teenagers toward their life purpose:

- Parenting, which is a dream common to millions of Christians, is one of God's most precious ordinations; it's a call into the ministry of helping your family know Jesus.

- It's an unparalleled privilege to have conversations with your children that help them discover and surrender to God's significant plan for their lives.

- God calls you to transformational work during your seasonal and long-term roles.

- God also calls you to a "This I Must Do" bold, far-reaching, specific assignment outside your home, often when you're empty-nested, *AK (After Kids)* and *WG (While Grandparenting)*—if not earlier.

Part 2 of this book contains six conversational exercises about life purpose. (Five conversations are parent-with-teenager; the sixth is between Jesus and each of you privately.) We'll be focusing on six best practices to help you discover and fulfill God's incredible plan for you. Or said more theologically accurate, we'll be focusing on six things you can do to *invite God to reveal* what additional life assignment—life mission— has been reserved especially for you. In those chapters, you'll discover suggestions for cooperating more strategically with the Creator of the universe to understand the rest of your life's work—to know what's next for you, after raising your children. **This chapter unpacks the logistics of how to engage your teenager in this entire process.**

When two Christians talk and listen

Anytime two Christians sit down to focus prayerfully on one single concept, like life purpose, for an uninterrupted period of time, God's almighty power is unleashed. Now, multiply that for the five critical conversations that you'll potentially have with your teenager, as well as a sixth one that each of you will have privately with Jesus. And add in the fact that you're creating a written document—a keepsake of shared answers, including a Lifetime Dream Statement and a Certificate of Surrender (which can also be downloaded from simplyyouthministry. com). Can you imagine the lifetime bond of trust, love, and respect that will be developed between you and your teenager during this God-led adventure?

Like you, your teenager longs to be used by God. If you invest in her emotionally and spiritually, and if you make a commitment to walk alongside her, listen to her, encourage her, and help her listen to God about the life mission that was assigned to her, you'll enjoy one of the richest experiences of your life.

God didn't intend for us to be lone rangers. Instead, we're expected to lean on one another to grow spiritually. In 1 Corinthians 3:6, Paul writes,

A Quick Note

The six chapters in Part 2 follow the content of the six-part, youth DVD curriculum *The Way I'm Wired: Discovering Who God Made ME to Be.* I wrote that video study to be used with church youth groups, Sunday schools, and schools-at-home, as well as at life purpose retreats for youth and similarly themed church camps. In other words, this book makes an excellent companion piece for parents whose teenagers are already going through the DVD material with an adult mentor.

For this parenting book, though, I don't make the assumption that you have the luxury of another adult coach involved in your process. Instead, this book gives you all the content and parenting prompts you need to talk to your teenager, without any outside support. It's been written as a stand-alone resource for you, as if it's just you and your teenager, with no other adult waiting to tag in.

I've given this book a parental perspective, loaded with real-life illustrations and discussion starters for private conversations and dinner table chats with your teenager.

I planted the seed in your hearts, and Apollos watered it, but it was God who made it grow. The key truth of that verse, of course, is that God caused the growth, while using others in the body of Christ to plant the seed and water it. Ecclesiastes 4:9-10 (written below the title of this chapter) complements that thought and tells us that there's great power in two people working together.

As you well know, teenagers can smell a fake, fraud, or setup. So, your genuine enthusiasm will speak volumes as you do the exercises and exchange personal discoveries with your teenager. And as "aha" moments begin to pop for you, you'll be living proof for your teenager that introspection and conversation are good for the soul.

How to invite your teenager to have a conversation with you

First of all, let me ask you a key question that will help you focus on the end result of inviting your teenager to discuss this book's topical exercises with you. *Do you believe that a few questions can change the course of a person's life or ignite a long-buried passion or create a more open relationship for future conversations?* If you do believe in the power God has assigned to simple conversations, then don't be shy about doing the inviting. Instead, get ready to marvel at the miracles you're about to witness.

Moving on to the inviting details: No one wants these conversations to be forced. When a teenager is required to talk with a parent about personal matters, the chat can turn into an ugly scene quickly, right? So, the key word in this section is *invite!* Not *force, coerce, beg, bribe,* or *manipulate by guilt.* (Although, truth be told, I did once bribe my son Andy with a little spending money to go to our church's summer camp for junior high students—and I'm sure glad I did! At that weeklong mountain camp, he committed his life to Jesus Christ. He was baptized when he got home, introduced his future wife to Christ in high school, and is now an awesome husband and father whose family loves Jesus dearly!)

The all-time master at inviting teenagers to chat is Doug Fields, who was my kids' youth pastor. He taught me that the fastest way to get a teenager to open up is to invite him or her to a Parent-Kid Dinner Night or for an unscheduled dessert outing alone. Stick hard and fast to the rule of not taking siblings with you, so you can more easily steer the conversation. Likewise, limit the outing to include only one parent, so it doesn't appear to be some type of intervention!

I can't tell you how quickly and easily that single, God-inspired, prayer-driven technique of sharing a meal or treat changed my parenting style. I discovered that the real art was to wait patiently until after they'd had a chance to relax, feel spoiled, and enjoy a few bites and sips of some of their favorite stuff. (Yes, the biggest hint I can share with you is to wait until their guard is down—until they're no longer expecting a Grand Inquisition!)

I went from demanding answers from my teenagers to politely and conversationally interspersing casual questions. The atmosphere was always relaxed, I was nonchalant, and the questions were simple, well-paced, and open-ended. Nothing like sounding off-the-cuff, instead of rehearsed, agenda-bound, hurried, and ready to pounce with a punishment:

- *Any fun stuff coming up?*

- *How's your boss been treating you?*

- *What's the gang up to these days? Is (specific friend or classmate) good?*

- *Any new drama, health issues, mission trip, parent trouble?*

- *You liking your new (Bible study, class partner, shoes, car, swim coach, and so on)?*

- *Do you need any dating advice from me? (This one is always good for a chuckle—and don't ever underestimate the miraculous effect of humor on any relationship!)*

After I got the hang of it, I was shocked that I didn't get any of the standard, on-the-fly answers that I had always gotten at home: *I dunno.*

Nuthin. Nope. No. Gotta go—see ya. Instead, stories flooded out of my teenagers like a perpetual lava flow. It was amazing. I still can't believe the quantity and quality of information they shared. And to sweeten the pot for you in a huge way, remember that in this conversational process, you'll actually have...

- your teenager's permission to chat

- a guiding script that keeps any surprise questions to a minimum

- ground rules like, *I dunno* and *nuthin* aren't answers

So, let's see how we can milk Doug's idea to help you be prepared to invite your teenager to participate in Part 2 of this book with you. (Remember to enlist prayer partners to ask God for the invitation to happen naturally and be received well; then stay alert to God-sent opportunities.) I offer these suggestions, knowing full well the enormous sacrifice and prayer commitment it will take to make any of them happen:

- **Prayerfully bold approach**
  Show your teenager this book. Be bluntly honest about what you're reading. Lead with a benefit statement *(discover your most unique life purpose—the reason you were born)* and follow quickly with the features of the process *(it's easy—we both mark our answers in different color ink on some charts in a book we share, and then I spring for dinner, while we compare our answers)*. Mention that he gets to pick 1-5 places for his favorite burger, tacos, pizza, or whatever is allowable food in your family. Close with an outcome statement, which is like another benefit *(knowing how God wired you can help you decide on your college major)*.

  If you only get quasi-interest, challenge your teenager to a "One Chapter Experiment" to see how it goes. Even if you get that first gig out of pity, take it—and pray like there's no tomorrow.

If your teenager seems excited about the process, schedule five Dinner Nights on Tuesdays from 6 to 7:15 p.m., for example, to discuss one chapter per week (Chapters 5-9). That's plenty of time to dine and discuss, assuming both of you have done the reading and exercises in advance. (Chapter 10 is an individual Surrender Exercise, so more on that later.)

- **Prayerfully moderate approach**
  Invite your teenager on an unexpected ice cream, yogurt, or fruit smoothie-type outing—and casually bring up one of the book topics you think will get her attention, without sending her running for cover. Throw out a question or two—and see how it goes from there. Or coolest of all, tell your teenager that you're testing yourself to see how well you know her—and ask her if she's interested in grading your book using a red pen. What teenager could resist grading Mom or Dad!

- **Prayerfully cautious approach**
  Tell your family that you're reading a book about life purpose and that you'd like to discuss a few of the topics over dinner meals, with each person around the table contributing their thoughts. If your teenager gets really excited about the discussions, ask if he'd like to share your book, so he can fill in his answers and then discuss them with you, perhaps, on the way to soccer practice on Saturdays.

- **Doubting Thomas approach**
  Leave the book lying around (bathrooms are your only hope) and pray that your teenager asks about it.

Logistics of Part 2

So, once you've got a warm body—I mean, *a willing participant*—how will the actual conversations with your teenager work? Here's what happens next.

- Read and do the exercises for Chapters 5-9. Use **black ink** to write your answers, but only answers you feel comfortable sharing with your teenager. (See "Set Boundaries" in this chapter for more about your comfort level in sharing.)

- **Optional:** If you'd like to see how well you actually know your teenager, use a pencil to indicate how you think he might respond about himself to the same questions you answered about yourself. Mark lightly in case you need or want to erase your guesses later. (Remember my story from the Introduction?)

- Share your book with your teenager and ask her to read and do the exercises for Chapters 5-9 at whatever pace you're scheduling your conversations, possibly one chapter per week. To help keep your answers distinct from each other's, ask her to use **red or blue ink**. The layout of each exercise actually makes that unnecessary, but it's still helpful for an at-a-glance overview and is a fun way to spotlight, in color, your teenager's individual God-wiring. (If you have more than one teenager, like my friends Shelley and Greg, who have five, you'll need to grab some purple, green, or other colored pens to keep everybody's answers straight. Or just assign each teenager to a different adult mentor who owes you a favor, while you take a long, deserved vacation! My prayers go with you if you have more than one teenager—for many reasons.)

- And finally, have five conversation-appointments with your teenager to compare your own answers about you with his final answers, as well as with any penciled-in guesses you may have made about him. (Use the proven conversational skills in Chapter 4 to make the process as effective as possible.)

Optional Best-Guesses

If you do choose to make tentative marks on behalf of your teenager, here's one word of caution: Never, ever make a notation on one of the exercises if it reflects your teenager in a bad light. That could be conversational suicide. So, when you see an exercise topic like *weaknesses,* make a note of your own weaknesses that you're comfortable sharing—but don't make any notation about your teenager's weaknesses. Wait until you can discuss the exercise verbally, sandwiched in between some easier topics or gentle-nature jabbering. And yes, I'll remind you of those few potential quicksand questions. Parent-to-parent, *I've got your back*!

Special Activity for Chapter 10: Personal Surrender Exercise

Chapter 10, *Surrendering All to Jesus*, is divided into two parts: the standard introductory teaching segment and the Personal Surrender Exercise. Read the teaching segment, and then ask your teenager to do so.

The purpose of the Personal Surrender Exercise is to surrender back to Jesus such things as your fears, motives, strengths, weaknesses, opportunities, threats, spiritual gifts, and lifetime dream.

There's no parent-teenager conversation related to the Surrender Exercise; that's between Jesus and each of you privately. This absence of discussion questions helps ensure that neither of you (A) will feel compelled to surrender something—anything—just to have something to discuss, or (B) will feel pressured to discuss something that's private that you felt led to surrender.

Here's a suggestion to mull over now, while you have some lead time: Consider arranging a special 45- to 60-minute solitude retreat for yourself and your teenager to do the exercise at the same time, but independent of one another. This private, uninterrupted time of quiet reflection can be in your own home or at one of your favorite places such as a park, lake, cabin, or beach. Prepare your heart now for this compelling yet simple exercise.

Note from my heart, as a mother and a professional Life Purpose Coach®

If you're doing the Surrender Exercise as an outing that takes you up into the mountains, for example, stay in safe proximity and within view of one another, and head home well before dark. And make sure you bring your own muted cell phone for emergencies—after you check for service-area coverage. Here's an abbreviated list of some of the most common mistakes that unprepared people have made. You'll want to avoid these mistakes before heading out with your precious cargo:

Forgetting to bring...

- Pen

- Reading glasses

- Sunscreen

- Sunglasses

- Hat or visor

- Water to stay hydrated

- Sweater or light jacket, if the weather is unpredictable

- Lawn chair or blanket to sit on, if ground tends to be wet

Choosing to bring...

- Sack lunch or sugary snacks that attract critters—large and small

- iPod to play worship songs and letting that become the focus

- Camera to take pictures of God's creation and letting that become the focus

- Cell phone that rings in the middle of the forest and gets answered

Other...

- Not having correct change for metered parking

- Forgetting to scope out the nearest restroom

- Going to a remote location without telling anybody their whereabouts

- Wearing designer shoes on slippery slopes or sandals on rocky ground

- Ignoring weather reports, storm clouds, and warnings for snow chains

- Getting heat stroke on a blistering day by not moving to the shade

Other than those few minor details, your teenager and you should be good to go!

15 Life Purpose Coach® Guidelines
for Successful Conversations

As we wrap up this chapter and get you closer to actually having a conversation with your teenager, I want to give you some essential techniques that I teach Life Purpose Coach® professionals to use with their clients worldwide. (It's worth noting that a Christian coach is one who's skilled at drawing out others in ways that enable them to self-discover what God has already designed and built into their lives. They help people live the lives they've only dreamed they could live.)

Prepare your heart to be a great coach to your teenager! You'll need these 15 guidelines, because people, including teenagers, can be unpredictable, stressed, moody, exhausted, and impatient. We live in a fast-paced world of entitlement with a mentality of *do it my way*. Nobody's perfect, and everybody's afraid of something. Besides, talking about God's plan can be downright intimidating. The most important thing you can do to have a successful conversation is to remember these truths:

You're *not* your teenager's...

- Prophet
- Coddler
- Problem solver
- Codependent best friend
- Genie-in-a-bottle
- Nagging parent
- Therapist
- Fixer or rescuer

You are your teenager's...

- Question asker
- Role model
- Missionary of hope
- Seed planter
- Objective listener
- Challenger
- Victory celebrator
- Fellow inquirer

Here's how to stay on track:

1. **Avoid the spotlight.** Be careful not to hijack the conversation unintentionally and steal the focus for yourself by interjecting unnecessary comments, constantly telling stories about your own life, or offering your opinion. Instead, step out of the spotlight, ask questions, and listen.

2. **Be a guide-on-the-side.** If a conversation gets bogged down or your teenager needs help in processing the material, act as a guide-on-the-side, not a sage-on-the-stage or a preacher-in-the-pulpit. You can *casually* ask a leading question like, "Why do you say that?" or "What if…?" or "If you could have a do-over, what would that look like?"

3. **Use appropriate doses of humor.** If you sense some tension of "we must do this assignment right" or "this is too hard," you can help your teenager relax into the process by interjecting some light humor.

4. **Encourage.** Recall your teenage years (you weren't so holy, huh?) so you can focus on how to minister to your teenager, who may need a smile or an extra word of encouragement. Your job/joy is to be a Barnabas—a Son (or Daughter) of Encouragement (Acts 4:36).

5. **Slow down.** Don't be tempted to rush the process because of a ticking clock. Rushing creates anxiety and stress that can shut down your teenager's ability to think. Just take it slow.

6. **Affirm.** Offer sincere, truthful affirmations to your teenager. Your conversations are intended to be a time of supportive brainstorming that can be fueled by much-needed, honest (not contrived) affirmation.

7. **Stay positive.** Your role is to walk alongside your teenager and offer support and hope. If you become a judge, jury, opinionated

critic, faultfinder, or dream squasher, the process is obviously doomed to fail. Stay positive.

8. **Prioritize.** These conversations must be a priority, not a nicety that can be canceled easily when your schedule gets overbooked. Rescheduling may be understandably necessary at times, but nothing will break the bond with your teenager faster than overbooking, standing him up, allowing constant interruptions, or becoming distracted.

9. **Set boundaries.** Some matters are private and can't be forced onto the table. With the help of the Holy Spirit, you and your teenager will know how much information to share with each other. It's very important that neither of you cross personal boundaries by sharing without thinking or by demanding answers from one another. Not everything has to be in writing to be known by God and you—or God and your teenager.

10. **Reconnect.** Watch for telltale signs that your relational bond has broken, including your teenager's harsh tone, folded arms, smirk, lack of eye contact, or disagreement with everything you say. Don't ignore those indicators. Instead, stop and repair the bond, even if that means taking a walk for 10 minutes or taking a break for 10 days. You won't get any pivotal work done, anyway, until you reconnect.

11. **Be patient.** People try to *invent* purpose because they grow tired of not having any answers. It's normal for people to try to control their destiny, but remind your teenager not to panic or get ahead of God. Encourage her to wait patiently for the Holy Spirit to reveal purpose—through prayer, Scripture, reflection, and conversations with other Christians. When there's confusion, we wait! Take a laughter break from the intensity by having some wholesome fun together or each with your own valued friends.

12. **Get perspective.** Don't forget God's perspective that your unique life purpose isn't really about you or what you want. (The same goes for your teenager.) You're both part of God's larger story of rescuing the world from darkness. Surrendering your lives and all your plans to the Ruler of the universe will put you both in a likely position to discover and fulfill the individual life mission for which you're wired.

13. **Nudge.** Your goal is to nudge your teenager to take a step in the direction the Holy Spirit is leading, not to dictate *shoulds* and *must do's* that will shut down the discussion. Use phrases and questions like these to move your teenager forward:

    - "Try it. If it doesn't work, you can try something else."

    - "Do a low-cost probe, a brief experiment, to see if you're on to something."

    - "Don't worry about trying to take a quantum leap; just take a baby step."

    - "What would you do now about your life mission, if you knew you couldn't fail?"

    - "If you're here and you want to be there, what are the steps in between?"

    - "Imagine the best possible scenario for yourself in X years. What first step can you take to get there?"

14. **Represent Christ.** Bottom line, your goal is to be like Jesus, who prayed with and for people, asked life-changing questions, listened, told stories, quoted Scripture, and personally submitted to God's will. (Skip the part about turning over tables in the temple courtyard or calling people *hypocrites*.)

15. **Breathe.** Reject the temptation to rescue, fix, console, or even protect your teenager from truth the Holy Spirit is revealing. Just breathe.

If Murphy's Law kicks in, and everything that could go wrong does go wrong, stay calm. Trust yourself, trust the Holy Spirit, trust the process, and remind your teenager that you trust him to do the same.

May God bless you as you help your teenager come alive with a passionate understanding of his life calling, his life mission! I pray that you'll...

- develop a greater, genuine trust with your teenager—a lifelong bond

- have fun and enjoy the process

- stay focused on the goal of the conversations with few detours

- graciously address conflict or resistance, if it arises

- press yourself for a commitment to fulfill God's plan for your life

- support your teenager's efforts to take steps toward her life purpose, too!

CHAPTER 3
THREE LARGE ELEPHANTS IN THE ROOM

Take delight in the Lord, and he will give you your heart's desires (Psalm 37:4).

Before we examine the specific dynamics of parent-teenager conversations, I must mention three things about a teenager's life purpose that you may think are like three large elephants hiding in the room that nobody wants to acknowledge. I wonder if you'd like to talk about these biggies:

- **1st Elephant:** *Can a teenager really discover his life purpose at such a young age?*

- **2nd Elephant:** *Even if my teenager thinks she has discovered her life mission now, won't it morph so much that it'll be unrecognizable and useless by the time she grows up?*

- **3rd Elephant:** *What if my teenager tries really hard to discover his life purpose but can't figure it out? Maybe it's best not to try, rather than face such discouragement.*

These are excellent questions, so let's expose those elephants, one at a time!

1st Elephant: Can a teenager really discover life purpose at such a young age?

God has orchestrated a season of life when children goof off, play dodgeball, build forts, ride bikes, enjoy Bible stories, and even learn to do chores and obey their parents. It's intended to be a fairly carefree age of innocence, where they trust their parents to meet all their needs. Those dear children long to hear general concepts from their parents and Sunday school teachers, like these:

- God loves you.

- God is all-powerful.

- God created you special.

- God wants you to tell others about Jesus.

As for teenagers, they're ready and eager to hear more specifics. They can be taught that God has a Master Plan for the world to be redeemed and that they're an integral part of that plan. In fact, they can accept that they have universal purposes and a unique purpose that are to be carried out in the name of Jesus—seasonally or long-term. They need to hear that God sends all sorts of sneak previews about their life mission and life message—that if they sit still quietly enough to hear God personally call them, they'll receive a revelation about the roles, goals, and lifetime dream that are specifically theirs.

And, oh, what a day of rejoicing that will be when they finally *get it!* They'll then have somewhere to direct all their young adult passion, as they gather resources, do research, build skill sets, establish a network, attend conferences with experts in their field, grow spiritually, choose a related college major, get an internship and job in their area of passion, and surround themselves with a prayer team—all on purpose, for a passionate purpose. They'll be filled with vision that gives them focus and builds their character. They'll be on the pathway to purpose.

Will life get in the way and put up roadblocks every chance it gets? Most definitely! But it'll be their passionate ache that is tucked away in their soul, even during years in a spiritual wilderness or of dealing with a life crisis that will give them hope and a reminder that God loves them enough to have assigned purpose to their lives.

Let Jeremiah weigh in about youth

We only need to read Jeremiah 1:7 to know that God's mission for individuals isn't limited by age. According to Bible scholars, Jeremiah was between 14 and 21 years old, when God told him: *"Don't say, 'I'm too young,' for you must go wherever I send you and say whatever I tell you."*

In fact, the entire passage (Jeremiah 1:4-12, 17) is so incredible that it deserves to be read to help show that God can make a life mission clear and imminent, regardless of age:

Jeremiah's Call and First Visions. *The Lord gave me this message: "I knew you before I formed you in your mother's womb. Before you were born I set you apart and appointed you as my prophet to the nations." "O Sovereign Lord," I said, "I can't speak for you! I'm too young!" The Lord replied, "Don't say, 'I'm too young,' for you must go wherever I send you and say whatever I tell you. And don't be afraid of the people, for I will be with you and will protect you. I, the Lord, have spoken!" Then the Lord reached out and touched my mouth and said, "Look, I have put my words in your mouth! Today I appoint you to stand up against nations and kingdoms. Some you must uproot and tear down, destroy and overthrow. Others you must build up and plant." Then the Lord said to me, "Look, Jeremiah! What do you see?" And I replied, "I see a branch from an almond tree." And the Lord said, "That's right, and it means that I am watching, and I will certainly carry out all my plans."… "Get up and prepare for action. Go out and tell them everything I tell you to say. Do not be afraid of them, or I will make you look foolish in front of them."*

So, yes, God does want teenagers to discover and begin to fulfill their life purpose. And you want that abundant life for your teenager, too.

> **2nd Elephant:** Even if my teenager thinks she has discovered her life mission now, won't it morph so much that it'll be unrecognizable and useless by the time she grows up?

Let's talk about that. Of course a teenager's most unique life purpose will morph somewhat as she matures emotionally and spiritually and is better able to understand God's strategic reasons for instilling a particular dream. Its core features and passions, though, will remain the same for all time. Would God confuse, frustrate, and play games with us by revealing one vision to us when we're young, only to say later on, "Oops, I changed my mind," and replace it with an all-new vision? No, our God isn't a God of confusion. We were born already fitting into the eternal plan of the Almighty—a plan that was crafted eons ago before the world began. Some have said that the process can feel like watching an old Polaroid photograph appear. It's foggy at first, but soon it's fully developed.

To illustrate this more concretely, let's take a look at one simple clue, out of dozens of clues that can act as a sneak preview from God. This particular clue is reflected in what teenagers think they want to be when they grow up.

What do teenagers want to be when they grow up?

Think back to your teenage years—what did you want to be when you grew up? Let me take a guess:

Perhaps it was a career in a "Helping" profession:

- Police officer, firefighter, or forest ranger

- Doctor, nurse, veterinarian, or speech therapist

- Teacher, counselor, or social worker

- Priest, nun, pastor, pastor's spouse, or choir director

- Missionary to an impoverished country

- President of your nation/country/company or a politician

- Soldier, military officer, pilot, or railroad conductor

- Scientist, geologist, or inventor

- Attorney or judge

- Author or motivational speaker

- Architect, contractor, builder, or heavy equipment operator

- Professional chef, artist, or musician

- Interior decorator, clothes' designer, or stylist

Perhaps it was a career in an "Exciting" profession:

- Triple threat performer: actor-singer-dancer

- Top-ranked athlete or race car driver

- Somebody famous, like a fashion model, radio broadcaster, or talk show host

- Hobbyist, like a professional surfer, skateboarder, or bicyclist

Nowadays, we can add these popular choices for professions:

- Technological genius

- Environmentalist

- Animal rights' activist

- Reality show star

- Rachael Ray–type of brand icon

What do all these careers have in common? They basically can be divided into two categories: (1) they help someone or some good cause, or (2) they fill a personal need for passion. How can a parent translate this career clue into usable, long-term, life purpose information? Simply focus on why your teenager wants a particular career. Listen to the heart and motive behind the career dream. For example, your teenager may want to be a...

- nurse, who comforts sick people so they aren't afraid.

- firefighter, who helps people escape physical danger.

- dancer, because she loves the freedom she feels when she dances.

- ski instructor, so he can be outdoors and teach what he loves.

- scientist, because she wants to find a cure for cancer to save lives.

- movie star, who's very well paid, famous worldwide, and talented.

- inventor, who gets to create something that makes people's lives better.

- forensic scientist, who takes down the bad guys with crime scene evidence.

How does this relate to life purpose?

God reveals a person's life purpose through, not only career dreams, but also other God-embedded particulars and life circumstances, such as…

• Passions	• Spiritual giftedness
• Talents/skills/abilities	• Hobbies
• Values	• Strengths/weaknesses
• Ministry	• Personality
• Relationships	• Life miracles
• Motives	• Character qualities
• Life experiences	• Opportunities

- Threats/fears
- Prayer life
- Heroes

...among other factors, many of which we'll target in this book! So, we can invite a revelation from God by asking a simple question that most people *never* ask:

"God, how would you like to use me—all of me—in your plan?"

That's the plain and simple formula! God has created your teenager (and you!) for a purpose. If you and your teenager are willing to ask that question about how your whole self can be used for God's purposes, both of you can expect a dependable revelation of your lifelong missions.

Here are some real-life illustrations of how this works in relation to just two factors (career dreams and passions), starting with my own story:

- **Katie:** As a child, I dreamed of being a missionary teacher in Africa and writing a book that gave people hope. I adored Sherlock Holmes mysteries and complicated jigsaw puzzles. Now I'm an author and the founder of a missionary-sending agency that helps people worldwide put together the puzzle of God's plan for their lives. I teach them that God never intended for their life purpose to be a big mystery or puzzle, and that it's possible to simply follow the clues (or put the puzzle pieces together) to invite the revelation.

- **Sally:** As a 27-year-old, she had a girl's dream of being a famous, professional dancer—and also of somehow expanding the peer-mentoring program at her high school to reach more teenagers. Today, she's completed her master's degree and is finishing her clinical hours to become a marriage and family therapist. She volunteers at church in the liturgical dance ministry. Sally daydreams, nearly daily, about opening a Christian camp for teenagers who need counseling and who'd also benefit from dance, music, and art therapy classes that she'd help teach. And of course, she prays for the camp to become famous worldwide!

- **Drew:** Now 34, he dreamed as a young boy about designing and building tree houses like he had in his backyard. His was a sanctuary for him, a place he could be alone to talk out loud about everything that was on his mind. As a teenager, he became clinically depressed after a drunk driver killed his girlfriend. At age 20, Drew chose to follow Jesus and soon donned a carpenter's tool belt to help his friends build a church. He says, "The hammering helped me get my anger out!" Today, with a powerful faith story of forgiveness, Drew has the privilege of being a men's retreat speaker who takes the guys on solitude retreats, where they can get away to talk to God out loud about everything that's on their mind. And he actually has built one very special tree house. He says, "It's not quite as cool as the Swiss Family Robinson house—but my little girl loves it."

Yes, a dream morphs somewhat as a person matures, but we'll always be able to see the threads that weave the tapestry together over the years. It's OK for your teenager to ask for a sneak preview or hint of a revelation regarding his unique mission. Receiving a glimpse of his future, far-reaching assignment will give him something to dream about during the daily-ness of life. And God knows that a dream and hope are more valuable than gold when navigating in this fallen world.

So, if your teenager dreams of saying, "I want to thank the Academy for this Oscar®," there's no need to discourage her passionate dreams. Instead, it's eternally important to encourage her to ask, "God, how would you like to use me—all of me—in your plan?"

I guarantee that her life mission will morph into a more incredible dream than she could ever dream for herself, with or without an Oscar®, if she learns to ask God to use her up. Nobody can out-dream God.

> 3rd Elephant: What if my teenager tries really hard to discover his life purpose but can't figure it out? Maybe it's best not to try, rather than face such discouragement.

I wish someone had shared with me that *me figuring out* my life mission puts all the pressure on me; whereas, *God revealing* my life mission makes me a recipient of whatever God feels is best for me to know at the time! With that fuller perspective, let's look at the reasons God might choose to withhold information—from a person of any age, whom I'll refer to as *you*.

Timing Issues:

- The people God is sending you to serve aren't ready for you— and you're being asked to wait, without any information or explanation.

- You may be overloaded by some of the current seasonal tasks you've been assigned at home, school, work, church, or in your community—with the critical duties that God has laid out for you in this season of life. Your mission right now simply might be to do your loving best with those responsibilities.

- You may be in crisis right now. You may be facing illness, injury, harm, death of a loved one, unemployment, financial trouble, betrayal, depression, discrimination, and/or recovery challenges— just to mention a few of the ways you may feel like you're dying physically, emotionally, or spiritually. You may be facing intense family dynamics or dire consequences for your actions. You may even be in a faith crisis due to a serious church or ministry upheaval.

Each of these crises requires your undivided attention to heal, which means that your basic life purpose is to move through the Five Stages of Dying. According to Dr. Elisabeth Kübler-Ross, those stages are Denial,

Anger, Bargaining, Depression, and Acceptance. In fact, your purpose is to move forward one small step at a time, so you won't get stuck in those stages. It's even important to move on eventually from the Acceptance Stage into an action phase.

Character Issues:

- God may want you, first, to address a character issue like pride, impatience, greed, or self-control that could greatly hinder your life mission. Yes, God called Saul on the Road to Damascus and blinded him to get his attention to do a remarkable 180-degree turnaround, but God's preferred method of launching a life mission is with your cooperation and preparation. You may need to work on issues such as fear, worry, procrastination, distractions, disorganization, or even laziness. Think of this as a gift of time, grace, and character building.

- God may know that you only want the *thrill of the hunt*, which is the thrill of hunting down your life purpose until you capture it— but that you don't really want to do the hard work of the mission itself. Curiosity may be driving you to discover your mission so you'll know what the exciting "IT" is, but God may know that you won't commit to it 100 percent. Let this insight lead you to a crisis of faith that will be a life-altering experience. Think of it as the gift of a *Motives' Do-Over* that is priceless.

Faith and Trust Issue:

- God may want you to pray fervently for a long time about your important life mission to increase your faith and trust. This often happens when the mission is so large that, to succeed, you'll need to believe—beyond a shadow of doubt—in the power, provision, and protection of God in all you're called to do.

And so, what do you say to your teenager who's anxious to hear God's plan? You can offer words of encouragement and a few suggestions, like these:

Because you're anxiously awaiting God's revelation, allow me to offer these specific words of encouragement to you heart-to-heart:

I know that waiting for your life mission to unfold can be very difficult. And because we really don't know how long you'll have to wait for God to reveal your life direction, it might be helpful if you...

- *Pray, as if you must wait a lifetime for God's plan to be revealed. Prepare your heart and character, as if you'll be launched tomorrow!*

- *In all circumstances, practice patience; it's a virtue that will serve you well forever.*

- *Seek balance in all areas of your life by prioritizing regularly to stay clear about how you want to spend your life.*

- *Take a baby step toward what you do know to be true about your life mission; you can always course-correct if you get a different impression about God's will.*

- *Don't worry. Rest. Be still. Be quiet. Take a break from the intensity of waiting by practicing the art of enjoying God's gift of life.*

I hope the three large elephants have been chased out of the room! God does work in our lives and in our teenagers' lives to unveil the best possible plan—at the best possible moment. Part 2 will walk you through exercises designed to help you and your teenager receive God's best.

CHAPTER 4

10 WAYS TO AMAZE YOUR TEENAGER WITH YOUR CONVERSATIONAL SKILLS!

The Lord was pleased that Solomon had asked for wisdom. So God replied, "Because you have asked for wisdom...I will give you a wise and understanding heart such as no one else has had or ever will have!" (1 Kings 3:10-12).

What do teenagers really want?

What do teenagers really want out of life—besides a car, tech toys, acceptance from their peers, and a date to the prom?

- Teenagers want to be heard. They appreciate the respect you show them when you listen to what they have to say—when you acknowledge that they have a voice that needs to be heard, especially on such an important topic as their life mission.

- Teenagers want their lives to matter. They have dreams, hopes, and longings—and they enjoy talking with someone who won't make fun of them and who will affirm them about how they can make a difference in the world.

- Teenagers want your attention. It's in their DNA. They're aware of your daily, personal investment in them, of how much unconditional love and support you offer them. They observe how much quality time you give them—even if they appear not to care about developing a relationship with you.

Your teenager may not know how to ask for your help with the daunting task of allowing God to reveal to him why he was born. But it can be one of your greatest-ever joys in life to offer. Who can he trust with these heart-issues, if not a loving parent who will actually walk alongside him, working through a step-by step process?

Ten skills are essential to having good conversations with your teenager and also with others the rest of your life. You already know most or all of these skills, so consider this a refresher course! These skills involve:

- Creating and maintaining a solid relationship

- Communicating effectively

- Moving the process along

If you succeed in doing even 10 percent of these things, your relationship will be deepened forever!

Skills #1-10

Skill #1: Invite the Holy Spirit to guide your conversation and establish a trusting relationship between you and your teenager. Rely on the Holy Spirit to give you eyes to see your teenager's needs, ears to hear what's really being said, and words to use during your conversations.

Jesus said, *"for the Holy Spirit will teach you at that time what needs to be said"* (Luke 12:12).

- **Establish a partnership between the Holy Spirit, your teenager, and you.** Ecclesiastes 4:12 tells us that a cord of three strands is not easily broken. This three-way partnership is critical to a successful conversation, and it's up to you to emphasize this relationship. A brief, simple prayer at the beginning of the session, inviting the Holy Spirit to partner with you, creates awareness that the work being done isn't solely up to you or your teenager.

- **Proceed in an atmosphere of trust.** Three human factors are critical to forming a bond of trust: kindness, a non-judgmental attitude, and confidentiality. Once trust is established, your teenager will know for certain that you're genuinely interested in moving him toward what's best for him. He'll be able to relax, be authentic, and talk to you as someone who cares about helping him explore and discover his life purpose. Encourage your teenager to trust the Holy Spirit, to trust you, to trust himself, and to trust the process.

Skill #2: Listen actively. The most important role you have is to be an active listener who hears all that's being said. This conversational skill requires listening to what the Holy Spirit is saying to you, as you listen to your teenager.

- **Listen reflectively.** Focus fully on your teenager and quietly reflect on what you're hearing. Think about the meaning of the words, not just about what brilliant insight you want to offer next. If you prayerfully take in what your teenager is saying, you won't get distracted.

- **Echo what you hear.** After you listen reflectively, echo what you hear by repeating what you think your teenager said. For example, you might say something like, "I heard you say that you're not happy with the part-time job you have after school and that you believe God has something else for you to do with your life right now. Is that correct?" Then your teenager can either agree or restate her thoughts. Echoing keeps you from putting your own interpretation on your teenager's words. It's key to understanding her.

Skill #3: Use the silence; don't fill it. Listening requires that you allow silence to be part of the conversation. The effective conversationalist respects the silence, rather than attempting to fill it. Silence can be a lightbulb illuminating something your teenager is processing, or it can be a laser beam indicating where he's hurting.

- **Allow your teenager time to process information.** Your teenager may be processing the question and deciding how he wants to explain his thoughts. Don't run ahead with constant words to try to fill in the uncomfortable space for him. If you do, your teenager may feel intimidated by your control or may lose track of his main point, just when he wanted to open up and share something important.

- **Realize that silence may be a self-defense mechanism.** Sometimes the silence could mean that the question has hit a nerve and your teenager is unwilling to answer. If so, after a short pause you can say something like, "I sense that you don't want to discuss that. Am I right?" This keeps the conversation on a positive track and shows respect for your teenager.

Skill #4: Mind the gap between the spoken and unspoken. This phrase—*Mind the gap*—originated in London as an official warning to railway passengers to watch out for the gap between the train door and the station platform.

In your conversation with your teenager, you may sense a gap between what's being said and what has been left unspoken. If you mind the gap—by paying close attention to it—you can spot positive and negative clues about what needs to be discussed.

- **Pay attention to positive clues.** For example, your teenager might talk broadly about her volunteer work at a homeless shelter. What she hasn't said is how passionate she is about it, but you notice a distinctly broad smile across her face—unlike any other response she's had so far. That's your cue to probe deeper and give her a chance to talk about the passion she feels. Often your teenager will feel genuinely honored that somebody cared enough to invite her to share more on a given topic.

- **Pay attention to negative clues.** For example, your teenager might say that she's doing fine, but her body language of crossed arms screams that she's closed off. She might say, "I had a late night—I'm too tired to think," to avoid discussing the truth about something. Or she might suggest a superhero-type action step in an attempt to mask her low self-esteem. Your role is to mind the gap prayerfully by probing gently for more information. You can say something like this in a kind tone, "So…what's going on?" Other times, it may be more appropriate to tuck the observation away until you have double-confirmation from the Holy Spirit to ask about it.

Skill #5: Initiate questions. Closely tied to listening skills are the questioning techniques you can use. Questions are powerful tools that help your teenager move forward, so remember to ask God for wisdom about them.

If you need wisdom, ask our generous God, and he will give it to you. He will not rebuke you for asking (James 1:5).

- **Ask questions that clarify a comment.** Get in the habit of asking questions that help you understand exactly what your teenager is saying. For example, you might ask, "Can you clarify that—give me a little more information?" This type of questioning helps your teenager know that you're actually listening and have a desire to understand more fully.

- **Ask questions that suggest a world of possibilities.** When you ask "What if?" questions, you're creating possibility thinking. This adds a fresh, thought-provoking perspective to a persistent problem your teenager is having, or it can challenge him to dream bigger. Either way, it becomes evident that your teenager will be stretched to do something that's only possible with God's power. Even if he ends up choosing a different or easier route, your goal of getting him to think outside the box has been initiated!

Skill #6: Use a simile to get a word picture. A simile is a comparison that uses *like* or *as* to paint a word picture. You can often prompt your teenager to uncover a timely truth by helping her paint a picture that's worth a thousand words.

- **Ask your teenager to give you a word picture using a simile.** If your teenager can't seem to find the words to describe a certain feeling or situation, ask her for a simile. (You may need to offer a brief definition or an example.) She might then say, "My low self-esteem makes me feel like an ant under a huge rock" or "Reaching my dream is as difficult as leaping the Grand Canyon." These types of answers will help you understand her better.

- **Give your teenager a word picture using a simile.** If your teenager is having trouble believing that God's love is always present, you might say something like, "God's love is like a mountain covered in fog. It's always present, even when the fog of life temporarily blocks the view."

Skill #7: Get to the heart of the matter. So far, you've learned to establish trust through the Holy Spirit, listen actively, allow silence, mind the gap, ask questions, and use similes. In the midst of all those good techniques, don't forget to check on your teenager's heart, emotions, and feelings. If he's the analytical type, he may not like you probing in this area, but it's crucial to his discovery about how he has been wired to fulfill God's plan.

- **Acknowledge your teenager's emotions.** Conversations deal with real life and messy heart issues. A teenager will be more likely to tell you what's in his heart when he's convinced that you really do care. When you acknowledge your teenager's feelings, he'll sense Christ's unconditional love through you. It's clear that you care when you say something like, "I know that experience must have been horrible for you."

Note: Empathizing (showing that you care) isn't taking on another person's problems as your own. You must know your boundaries. If you have a bent toward shouldering the burdens of others, guard against it with your teenager.

- **Ask a heart question.** The most well-known heart question is, "How does that make you feel?" If you get a blank stare to such a *feelings* question, just be patient and rephrase it with something like: "If you could pay a fee to make a feeling go away, how much would you pay to eliminate which feeling?" He may say, "I'd pay a million bucks to get rid of my guilt" or "I'd give all the money in the world to eliminate my feeling of not being smart enough or good enough." His answer will help you get to the heart of the matter fast. (Another great question is, "So, what's blocking you?") Remember: *I dunno* and *nuthin* aren't answers! Probe for more.

Skill #8: Nudge to move forward. Your teenager may get stuck at key times, which could delay God's revelation of her boldest life purpose, but don't panic; that's quite normal. For some, stubbornness is a protective measure to ward off fear of commitment, fear of failure, or fear of being out of their comfort zone. For others, the hesitation is because they've never been encouraged to move toward their dreams, so they're truly confused about how to go forward. Your role is to nudge your teenager toward taking a baby step or two—or three!

May he grant your heart's desires and make all your plans succeed (Psalm 20:4).

- **Ask action-oriented questions.** Action-oriented questions help those who are frozen in a state of mental paralysis or who seem to be getting confused, sidetracked, or over-committed. In these instances, you can ask your teenager a simple question like, "What can you do to lessen your depression by 25 percent?" or "What baby step can you take to realign your thoughts with God's purpose and hopes for your life?"

- **Strategize next steps to take.** In addition to inviting your teenager to name some action steps that will move her toward her life mission, you can brainstorm with her to capture a few great ideas. This can be fun for a few minutes, if she's receptive.

  Note: It's important that you guard yourself against too much ownership of the goals, action steps, and results that belong to your teenager. Remind her to draw upon the strength of the Holy Spirit and to encourage her, but it isn't up to you to do the work for her.

Skill #9: Navigate change. Change is an inevitable result of the plans and goals your teenager has discussed with you. These changes are the crux of the conversational process, but they're almost never welcomed because they can be difficult to make. God requires us, however, to change our thoughts, words, and actions to be conformed to Christ's ways. Your role is to help your teenager scope out possible options for how to navigate the rough waters of change.

- *Look Out:* **Recognize that change is often difficult.** An effective conversationalist will verbalize that habits aren't easily changed. It's hard, for example, for people to quit smoking, lose weight, stop gossiping, or forgive someone. Let your teenager know that you realize change can be difficult, but that you'll cover him in prayer.

- *Look In:* **Replace the negative with the positive.** When your teenager decides that he needs to change something in his life, help him find a positive replacement for the negative behavior. For example, if your teenager worries habitually about his grades, he could replace that worry with memorizing a passage about trusting God—and joining a study group that ends each session in prayer.

- *Look Up:* **Celebrate victories.** Not everyone allows himself a celebration of his accomplishments or of his recovery from setbacks, so your role is to applaud your teenager's effort and commend his success. And you may need to challenge him to take a laughter break, go on an outing, or think of a different healthy reward. Point him again to the One who most wants to celebrate with him.

Skill #10: Conclude with intentionality. Take a few minutes to end well. It'll bless your teenager and speak volumes about your intention to serve her during this series.

- **Ask your teenager to summarize her insights at the end of your conversation.** When your teenager hears herself giving a recap of the discussion, it helps her see how the session has been productive and is moving her forward—one action step at a time, toward her life mission.

- **Challenge your teenager and yourself to memorize the Scripture verse.**

- **Affirm with a positive statement about who your teenager is in Christ.** To affirm your teenager, you might mention her obvious love for Jesus and her readiness to be all God created her to be. This helps bring her back to the sweet spot of her relationship with Christ, the reason she's having the conversations in the first place. It's a reminder that, in Christ, she's free to learn, grow, and reach for her potential. Your affirming remark may be the gift of encouragement your teenager needed more than anything else. You may never fully know, until you get to heaven, how much your words meant to her or how they affected her life.

- **Close with a brief, personalized prayer.** You'll know what to pray (in addition to or instead of the suggested prayer) by sensing through the Holy Spirit what your teenager needs you to pray on her behalf. Assure your teenager that you'll be praying for her.

Remember that the point of this chapter wasn't to stress you out with rules or make you feel that it's too difficult to proceed. The point was to help you see that it's just a conversation! It's a time of listening attentively to your teenager and responding in a prayerful, affirming, undistracted, and encouraging way. May you be blessed to be a blessing as you do so.

PART 2

PARENT-
TEENAGER
CONVERSATIONS

CHAPTER 5

UNDERSTANDING YOUR SPIRITUAL GIFTS, BEST QUALITIES, AND FINEST VALUES

God has given each of you a gift from his great variety of spiritual gifts. Use them well to serve one another (1 Peter 4:10).

Tsunami Evacuation Warning

I temporarily moved to Maui to write this book in a serene environment. Ah, how our best-laid plans often go wrong, right? Not long after the move, the blare of outdoor sirens woke me up and alerted all residents that we were under a tsunami evacuation warning. An 8.8 earthquake had rattled Chile, and waves were racing across the Pacific Ocean, threatening Hawaii.

According to the National Weather Service, the first 8-foot wave was projected to hit the island chain shortly after 11 a.m. in a series of nine waves that might be traveling up to 600 mph on any given surge. As the governor declared a state of emergency, helicopters took to the sky to deliver urgent warnings via loudspeakers.

Cars began to line up 15-deep at gas stations so families could make a mad dash for the hills and stay mobile during the recovery process. Residents stormed into supermarkets to stock up on water, canned food, and batteries, in anticipation that our utilities would be turned off for days or weeks. All the fast-food places, like McDonald's and Burger King, quickly shut down. We heard that the leprosy patients on the island of Molokai were all moved to higher ground, and I was being evacuated, as well, to my pastor's home up on the hillside.

I was out the door in the recommended footwear—tennis shoes—with my family photos, laptop, and travel Bible, along with some food, water, toilet paper, fully charged cell phone, candles, matches, radio, flashlight with extra batteries, and a change of clothes, including a nighttime jacket. The locals also told me to take my snorkel, goggles, water socks, bike helmet, and wrist guards in case we found ourselves swimming in the ocean with flying objects like bicycles!

Although the warning was lifted officially at 1:38 p.m. after no reported damage, it wasn't before this Tsunami Mamma had called and texted her two children and their spouses, along with other family members and a friend to tell them: *I luv u*. It was during those few hours of uncertainty that I knew—and hope I'll never forget—the incredible importance of personal relationships.

The tsunami scare also made me stop to think about this book. Was I, for example, practicing what I was preaching and writing? Was I fully engaging—on my own unique life mission—all the strengths, opportunities, spiritual gifts, qualities, values, and relationships I had been given? Was I persevering past roadblocks and expecting miracles to carry me to the finish line? Was I self-sabotaging my assignment with sin, poor motives, or poor use of my time? Was I being courageous in the face of external threats? Was I on-track with my own Lifetime Dream Statement? Was I fully surrendered to God, come what may? All things that I would be asking you as readers to address!

I'm grateful that the tsunami caused me to take stock of my life. And I pray that God will use this book to move you and your teenager forward toward your distinct life missions as if you're both responding to a life-awakening warning that's resounding out of heavenly loudspeakers!

Let's dig in now by looking at why you were born, what's next for you, and what incredible life assignment (in addition to parenting) has been reserved especially for you! After you work through the materials, you can invite your teenager to do the exercises and discuss these topics with you. Perhaps that sounds familiar, like the announcement flight attendants make to tell you to secure your oxygen mask first, before attempting to assist your child!

Of the six best practices we'll address to help you discover and fulfill the unique plan God designed specifically for you, the most foundational is this first one: **Understanding Your Spiritual Gifts, Best Qualities, and Finest Values**.

Tip about how to cooperate with God's plan: If I understand my spiritual gifts, best qualities, and finest values, I'll see undeniable evidence regarding the specific life work God has assigned me. (And the same is true for your teenager!)

How to Have a Conversation With Your Teenager

After you've completed all three exercises in this chapter, follow these guidelines:

1. On the "Spiritual Gifts" and "Best Qualities" exercises, you have the option of using light, tentative pencil markings to indicate how you think your teenager might answer. However, for the "Finest Values" exercise, the instructions will indicate that you're *not to guess your teenager's answers*, which might not be all pretty!

2. As you hand off this book to your teenager, encourage him to read the opening remarks of the chapter and the topical explanations that are prior to the exercises. Or you can offer to give a brief overview of this chapter's topics and to answer any related questions.

3. Ask your teenager to use red or blue ink to do the three exercises, leaving any incorrect pencil notations—for a fun, lively comparison.

4. When it's time to kick off your parent-teenager conversation, open your time by personalizing a brief prayer, like this:

    Holy Spirit, we invite you to guide our conversation and establish a trusting relationship between us. We ask for your wisdom as we explore how we've been wired with spiritual gifts, best qualities, and finest values—all bold indicators of God's specific plan for us. Amen.

5. Discuss the Reflection Questions for all three exercises, treasuring the God-centered time with your teenager.

Note: Your teenager and you may require an extra measure of grace during the "Finest Values" exercise, so dole it out freely to both of you, as Christ does.

Understand my spiritual gifts

Spiritual gifts are those few, very special attributes that have been wired into you through the grace of God to be specifically used in blessing the body of Christ for a particular season. Think of them as birthday presents from the Holy Spirit, because they were given to you at the time of your spiritual birth—when you joined the family of God. (Other gifts are added or subtracted along the way, depending on your need for them in doing the work you've been assigned—and your faithful use of them.) First Corinthians 12:7 tells us that spiritual gifts are given for the benefit of serving others. So, just to be clear, non-Christians don't have spiritual gifts.

A spiritual gift isn't simply something you can do well if you try really hard. It's something that comes natural for you; it's nearly effortless. For example, do you enjoy any of these particular spiritual gifts mentioned in Romans 12:6-8:

- Speaking out with great faith
- Teaching
- Giving
- Showing kindness

- Serving others
- Encouraging
- Leading

Sure, some of those, like teaching or leading, seem like regular ol' talents, skills, or abilities, right? But when you've been commissioned by God to use them specifically for kingdom work, they become spiritual gifts. Ephesians 4 tells us that when spiritual gifts such as administration, hospitality, or martyrdom (bet you wish you had that one!) are used by the members of a church, then the entire church body matures spiritually.

When you receive two or three gifts, we refer to that as a "spiritual gift mix." Studying your spiritual gift mix is a great way to know the purpose in your life that will have the greatest and most far-reaching impact on the world (beyond parenting, of course). Why is that true? Because God grants divinely ordained spiritual gifts to Christians—with the expectation that we'll use them to the greatest degree possible to influence others. It's God's ingenious way of equipping us for our well-orchestrated life mission outside our own home.

And most importantly, if we remember that we're only stewards of these powerful spiritual gifts, we won't become puffed up about them.

Exercise #1: My Spiritual Gifts

Instructions: Check the gifts you feel are in your spiritual gift mix.
(□ **Parent** □ **Teenager**)

Spiritual Gifts

P	T		P	T	
□	□	Administration/Organization	□	□	Apostleship/Modern Missionary
□	□	Craftsmanship/Skilled Hands	□	□	Encouragement/Exhortation
□	□	Discernment/Keen Judgment	□	□	Faith
□	□	Evangelism	□	□	Healing Miracles
□	□	Giving	□	□	Intercessory Praying
□	□	Hospitality	□	□	Leadership
□	□	Knowledge/Wisdom	□	□	Lifetime Celibacy
□	□	Martyrdom	□	□	Mercy/Compassion
□	□	Pastor/Shepherd	□	□	Prophecy/Blessed Sayings
□	□	Service/Helps	□	□	Tongues/Interpretation
□	□	Voluntary Poverty	□	□	Communication: Drama, Internet/Computers, Music, Photography, Preaching, Teaching, Video, Visual Arts, Writing

Reflection Questions about your spiritual gifts:

1. Which top two or three spiritual gifts do you feel you've been given to serve the body of Christ? Why?

2. In what way could you use one of your gifts now or later to do God's work on earth?

Understand my best qualities

It's important to know your best qualities (finest character traits) so you can maximize them for God's work. Would your most supportive family members and closest friends say that you have one of these qualities: affirming, calm, forgiving, or respectful?

Every minute of every day, someone is choosing a friend, spouse, employee, mentor, or counselor based on the qualities of loyalty, honesty, reliability, tact, punctuality, and/or trustworthiness. And remarkably, God has instilled just the right qualities in your personality for you to pursue your life's work and collect an eternal reward. That's some more of God's *equipping*.

Understand my finest values

This topic is straightforward because the word *values* says it all. Your *values* tell everyone what you consider *valuable*, important, useful, or desirable—especially regarding your personal conduct. *Core values are guiding principles—whether positive or negative—that indicate what you hold in high esteem.* They're the moral and ethical rudders that steer your ship.

It's important to evaluate your core values closely to see how many of them are Christ-honoring and which ones would outlive all others as your finest values. This will help you better understand how they support or interfere with your long-term life mission. Ask yourself what you value most. Would you say it's any of these: freedom, truth, power, fun, fame, control, or travel?

Once you look over the complete list of positive and negative core values, you'll have to decide if "fun," for example, is the value that will help you accomplish the task you were put on earth to complete. *Fun* would actually be a perfectly fine value for a Christian comedian who uses the stage to spread the good news about Jesus.

Exercise #2: My Best Qualities

Instructions: Check or write your five or six best qualities you believe you possess that can help you be and do all God desires.
(□ **P**arent □ **T**eenager)

Best Qualities

P	T		P	T	
□	□	Able to Admit Mistakes	□	□	Able to Say I'm Sorry
□	□	Affirming/Encouraging	□	□	Authentic/Genuine
□	□	Brave	□	□	Calm
□	□	Confident	□	□	Cooperative
□	□	Courageous	□	□	Creative
□	□	Empathetic/Caring	□	□	Energetic
□	□	Fair	□	□	Focused
□	□	Forgiving	□	□	Friendly/Kind/Loving
□	□	Funny	□	□	Generous
□	□	Grateful/Thankful	□	□	Honest
□	□	Humble	□	□	Imaginative
□	□	Inspirational	□	□	Intuitive/Instinctive
□	□	Joyful/Happy	□	□	Logical
□	□	Loyal	□	□	Nurturing
□	□	Obedient	□	□	Observant
□	□	Passionate	□	□	Patient
□	□	Persistent	□	□	Persuasive
□	□	Positive	□	□	Prayerful
□	□	Punctual	□	□	Reasonable
□	□	Reliable	□	□	Respectful
□	□	Responsible	□	□	Risk Taker
□	□	Strategic	□	□	Teachable
□	□	Trustworthy	□	□	Vulnerable
□	□	Other:	□	□	Other:

Reflection Questions about your best qualities:

1. Which five or six best qualities has God wired into you, and how have you used one of your qualities for good?

2. In what way do several of your best qualities give you a possible hint about what your unique life purpose might be?

Exercise #3: My Finest Values

Instructions: Reflecting on all areas of your life (personal, family, friendships, school, job, spiritual walk, ministry, community, and life contribution), check or write your core values—without trying to choose what sounds like a great Christian value. *Don't try to guess your teenager's answers. Not all are pretty!* (□ **P**arent □ **T**eenager)

Core Values

P	T		P	T	
□	□	Accountability	□	□	Adventure
□	□	Appearance	□	□	Authenticity
□	□	Being Right	□	□	Being Thanked
□	□	Cleanliness	□	□	Comfort
□	□	Competition	□	□	Confidentiality
□	□	Control/Structure	□	□	Courage
□	□	Diversity/Equality	□	□	Duty/Obligation
□	□	Earthly Reward	□	□	Eternal Reward
□	□	Excellence/Quality	□	□	Faith/Trust in God
□	□	Fame/Prestige	□	□	Freedom
□	□	Fulfillment	□	□	Fun/Entertainment
□	□	Goal Completion	□	□	Health/Fitness
□	□	Healthy Relationships	□	□	Holiness
□	□	Humor	□	□	Independence
□	□	Innovation/Creativity	□	□	Intelligence
□	□	Justice/Fairness	□	□	Life Balance
□	□	Lifelong Learning	□	□	Pain Relief
□	□	Perfection	□	□	Perseverance
□	□	Physical Strength	□	□	Pleasure
□	□	Popularity/Reputation	□	□	Possessions
□	□	Power	□	□	Predictability
□	□	Recognition	□	□	Relationship With Jesus
□	□	Safety	□	□	Significance/Purpose
□	□	Simplicity	□	□	Spiritual Growth
□	□	Success	□	□	Teamwork
□	□	Truth	□	□	Unconditional Love
□	□	Wealth	□	□	Other:

Reflection Questions about your finest values:

1. Which are your top five or six core values? Why do you say that?

2. In what way could several of your finest values be part of God's wiring for your future life mission?

3. How might one or some of your values interfere with God's best for your life?

Will You?

Could God have been speaking to you through these exercises about several critical next steps of utilizing your spiritual gifts, best qualities, and finest values to bless your life mission? Will you, in preparation for your most far-reaching assignment, move forward using the undeniable truths you've begun to gather about yourself? Starting now, how will your prayerful insight about how you're wired affect your day-to-day living and (if you have a glimpse of it already) your unique life mission?

To wrap up your parent-teenager conversation with intentionality:

- **Encourage your teenager to summarize her insights, by asking a question like this:** *Starting now, how will your prayerful insight about how you're wired with spiritual gifts, best qualities, and finest values affect your day-to-day living and (if you have a glimpse of it already) your unique life mission?*

- **Challenge your teenager and yourself to memorize the verse at the beginning of this chapter.**

- **Challenge your teenager and yourself to do this special homework assignment for the entire series:** Ask the Holy Spirit to reveal to you a *life verse*—a Scripture that affirms your unique life mission! You never know whether the verse or mission will be revealed first, but they'll complement one another perfectly. Memorizing and reflecting often on your life verse will help you as you move down the pathway to purpose.

- **Affirm with a positive statement about who your teenager is in Christ.**

- **Close by personalizing a brief prayer, like this:**

  God, it's incredible that you'd design a life mission for us that's supported directly by our spiritual gifts, best qualities, and finest values. In fact, it's mind-boggling how you can make it all work together for your glory and for the good of those we're called to serve. Thank you for such an intricately wired plan. In Jesus' name we pray. Amen.

CHAPTER 6

RETHINKING YOUR MOTIVES, RELATIONSHIPS, AND USE OF TIME

People may be pure in their own eyes, but the Lord examines their motives (Proverbs 16:2).

Swimmers' Chant

I grew up in a middle-class family with eight kids and dedicated parents who both worked hard to give us everything we needed and most of what we wanted. But one thing we didn't have in sunny Southern California was a swimming pool in our backyard. I'm not complaining—just giving you the facts so I can ask you a question about what you'd have done in this real-life situation:

Would you have kissed up to the rich, snooty, new girl in your class, Christy, who had a huge, backyard pool that was calling your name as the hot summer months drew near?

Yes? No? Maybe? Well, my sisters and I did schmooze with that bratty, hoity-toity Christy every chance we got. We said such lovely things to her face, lavishing her with compliments about everything—but behind her back, we chanted our deceptive motive for being nice to her:

We love you, Chris-is-ty. Oh yes we do.

We love you, Chris-is-ty, and your P-O-O-L, too!

Our motive for being kind to Christy wasn't so pure, huh? In fact, our motive was downright wrong. Let's jump off the high dive now into the deep end of this book with several such topics as this! It's all for the sake of learning to bring glory to God, as your teenager and you both submit to the matchless call on your lives.

Best Practice #2

Still want to investigate the reason God put you on earth—even though it's not as easy as you might have thought it would be? If so, it's time to look at this best practice that will help you invite God to reveal your life mission: **Rethinking Your Motives, Relationships, and Use of Time**. (After you work through the materials, you can invite your teenager to discuss these topics with you.) This suggested lifelong habit might be the most overlooked key to success on your distinct life mission because it cuts to the root of God's expectations for you.

Tip about how to cooperate with God's plan: If I rethink my motives, relationships, and use of time, I'm better prepared to answer God's call on my life. (And the same is true for your teenager!)

How to Have a Conversation With Your Teenager

After you've completed all three exercises in this chapter, follow these guidelines:

1. Don't try to guess any of your teenager's answers.

2. As you hand off this book to your teenager, encourage him to read the opening remarks of the chapter and the topical explanations that are prior to the exercises. Or you can offer to give a brief overview of this chapter's topics and to answer any related questions.

3. Ask your teenager to use red or blue ink to do the three exercises.

4. When it's time to kick off your parent-teenager conversation, open your time by personalizing a brief prayer, like this:

   Holy Spirit, we rely on you to give us eyes to see what encouragement and grace we each need during this conversation. Thank you for being available to us to offer insight and guidance regarding our motives, relationships, and use of our time. This we pray. Amen.

5. Discuss the Reflection Questions for all three exercises, treasuring the God-centered time with your teenager.

Note: If you start to feel like the "judge and jury" while you're listening to your teenager, dismiss those thoughts immediately.

Rethink my motives

God cares deeply about your motives, which are your conscious and unconscious reasons for what you do and don't do. This exercise will help you appreciate your right motives and reconsider your wrong motives, so you can be more real—more authentic—in your everyday life and your kingdom work. It may even surprise you.

For example, are you more likely to…

- give a gift out of love for a person, or simply to prompt a gift in return?

- offer a prayer request for a friend to enlist prayer warriors, or simply to gossip?

- volunteer at a hospital to serve the patients out of love for Jesus, or simply to clock-in service hours or get kudos?

- attend small group to fellowship and learn more about your Christian walk, or simply to satisfy an obligation—or show off your new outfit?

It may be OK to hide certain things, like when a manly-man wears makeup to disguise a zit or when a soldier wears a camouflage uniform to hide from the enemy. But let's face it, all cover-ups create an illusion; they purposefully deceive people. They create an outward appearance to create a better payoff than what the truth will pay. (A manly-man gets the date; a soldier gets the victory.)

God is already aware of the inside scoop about everything you think and do. In fact, these verses tell us:

> *"God examines every heart and sees through every motive"*
> *(1 Chronicles 28:9 The Message).*

> *Put me on trial, Lord, and cross-examine me. Test my motives and*
> *my heart (Psalm 26:2).*

> *People may be pure in their own eyes, but the Lord examines their*
> *motives (Proverbs 16:2).*

Are you ready to begin living a more authentic (real, bona fide, genuine) life by thoroughly understanding your motives and your reasons for doing and not doing things?

Key Idea #1: God abhors wrong motives.

- We've all said, "I'm sorry" to ease our guilt.

- Or perhaps we've tithed to feel good about giving money to the church.

- Or maybe we've even attended an event to be seen with the "in crowd."

God is an expert at spotting self-serving motives that may appear innocent to others. Consider the person who donates money to a worthy cause, but does so for personal recognition rather than to help others. Matthew 23:27-28 tells us how God felt about the Pharisees, whose motive was to *appear* holy:

"Hypocrites! For you are like whitewashed tombs—beautiful on the outside but filled on the inside with dead people's bones and all sorts of impurity. Outwardly you look like righteous people, but inwardly your hearts are filled with hypocrisy and lawlessness."

Whoa! I'm so glad Jesus was talking to real hypocrites, and not to me! But wait a minute. We all try to appear righteous, while we're full of hypocrisy. For example, think about one wrong motive you may have had for serving on a committee. Or think about a poor motive, like jealousy, anger, or guilt, that led you into another sin, such as theft, abuse, or lying. Bottom line: Wrong motives destroy us and lead to other secret sin.

Key Idea #2: Pure and right motives always give glory to God.

Let's test out the idea that pure and right motives always give glory to God. Think about this: What is a right motive for a single woman wanting to date a single man? If her motive is because the guy is great arm candy—where's God in that action? If her motive, instead, is to meet a Christ-like mate, then bam! She's on the right track.

Let's try another one: What might your motive be for giving a speech about recycling? If your motive is to save the planet—well, that's a great secular motive, but it's called humanism, meaning we do good things for human beings because we want to be a good person. If your motive, instead, for giving that speech is to honor your commitment to God, as a steward of creation, then bam! You're on the right track.

So, just to be clear: **Motives that indicate you're a good, awesome, and decent human may be in a gray area spiritually, simply because they don't pass the litmus test of** *doing it for the glory of God.*

Key Idea #3: Your motives impact your life mission.

What if you begged God with this prayer: "God, if you'll please, please tell me my exciting purpose in life, I promise I'll work really hard on it." If your motive for that prayer is curiosity, then once your curiosity is satisfied and the excitement dies down, you won't follow through on the hard work of completing the mission that was crafted for you before you were born. Your true motive is selfish: to feel the thrill of discovering God's plan, not to answer a call to serve.

We don't want to be careless about our motives. And we can be thankful that God will help each of us become honest people who can be entrusted with a challenging life mission.

Exercise #1: My Motives

Instructions: On the next two pages, draw a line from each *Positive or Negative Action* toward the entire Primary Motive Grouping that typically fits your motive. It's OK to point toward two motive groups for some of the actions, but doing that more than a few times will skew your results. If you've never done a particular action (like *steal*), or if you prefer to skip it, just skip it. *Notice the extra Motives Chart for your teenager. Don't try to guess your teenager's answers!*

Hint: It will make the exercise and discussion questions easier if every time you draw a line toward a grouping, you also put a check mark to the far right of that grouping.

Positive or Negative Action (Parent)

Ask for forgiveness

Ask for prayer for myself

Ask for prayer for someone

Attend a family event

Be extra kind to a friend

Befriend a homeless person

Cheat on a relationship

Cheat on a test

Criticize someone

Discover my life purpose

Do a household chore

Encourage/affirm someone

Fast from something

Flatter/charm someone

Get an "A" in a class

Give a nice gift

Give a speech

Gossip

Go to a party or event

Go to small group/church

Go to work

Hold an elected office

Judge someone

Lie about something

Make a donation

Mentor someone

Say, "I'm sorry"

Send a card

Serve on a committee

Stand up for a cause

Stand up for myself

Steal something

Talk to someone about Jesus

Tithe 10 percent of my income

Other Action:

Primary Motive Grouping (Parent)

I'm Supposed To
- Avoid disappointing someone
- Satisfy an obligation/a *should*
- Reduce shame or guilt
- Smooth over awkward situation

I People-Please to Fit In and Belong
- Be accepted into the "in crowd"
- Feel normal, not odd
- Be liked by peers and others
- Improve damaged reputation

I'm Alive and I Matter, So Notice Me
- Beat out competition/win
- Cause drama
- Feel passion or thrill
- Receive a reward/prize/kudos
- Brag or impress
- Feed my ego/get attention
- Get sympathy or a laugh
- Show off talent/beauty/body

I Protect Myself
- Avoid ugly confrontation
- Decrease boredom
- Guard turf
- Mask or stuff down feelings
- Avoid physical pain
- Feel good emotionally (less hurt)
- Hide my inadequacies to feel safe
- Pay back or get revenge

I Can Affect or Control You
- Cause embarrassment/pain
- Create indebtedness to me
- Stir up trouble or provoke
- Create codependency
- Manipulate or exploit
- Wield power

God Reigns
- Be a good steward of what I have
- Be in relationship with Jesus
- Care for God's Temple—my body
- Enlist prayer warriors
- Give glory to God
- Love as Jesus first loved me
- Obey the Ruler of the universe
- Spread good news of the gospel
- Use my gifts for the kingdom
- Become more Christ-like
- Be righteous (do what's right)
- Discover truth/wisdom
- Follow God's plan for my life
- Have Christ-like relationships
- Mature in my faith
- Represent Jesus to someone
- Take care of those entrusted to me
- Work as if working for the Lord

I Like to Investigate and Learn
- Experiment/discover/research
- Offer a new opinion/method
- Master a new skill
- Satisfy curiosity

I Want It, Need It, or Deserve It
- Get rich
- Go wherever I want
- I'm exempt from the rules
- Get what I've worked for/paid for
- Have nice things/satisfy desires
- I'm entitled to better treatment

I Respect People and Our Planet
- Make a difference
- Offer hope/love/gratitude
- Reduce suffering/meet a need
- Offer comic relief
- Open lines of communication
- Show respect/give honor

Other Motive: _____

Positive or Negative Action (Teenager)

Ask for forgiveness

Ask for prayer for myself

Ask for prayer for someone

Attend a family event

Be extra kind to a friend

Befriend a homeless person

Cheat on a relationship

Cheat on a test

Criticize someone

Discover my life purpose

Do a household chore

Encourage/affirm someone

Fast from something

Flatter/charm someone

Get an "A" in a class

Give a nice gift

Give a speech

Gossip

Go to a party or event

Go to small group/church

Go to work

Hold an elected office

Judge someone

Lie about something

Make a donation

Mentor someone

Say, "I'm sorry"

Send a card

Serve on a committee

Stand up for a cause

Stand up for myself

Steal something

Talk to someone about Jesus

Tithe 10 percent of my income

Other Action:

Primary Motive Grouping (Teenager)

I'm Supposed To
- Avoid disappointing someone
- Satisfy an obligation/a *should*
- Reduce shame or guilt
- Smooth over awkward situation

I People-Please to Fit In and Belong
- Be accepted into the "in crowd"
- Feel normal, not odd
- Be liked by peers and others
- Improve damaged reputation

I'm Alive and I Matter, So Notice Me
- Beat out competition/win
- Cause drama
- Feel passion or thrill
- Receive a reward/prize/kudos
- Brag or impress
- Feed my ego/get attention
- Get sympathy or a laugh
- Show off talent/beauty/body

I Protect Myself
- Avoid ugly confrontation
- Decrease boredom
- Guard turf
- Mask or stuff down feelings
- Avoid physical pain
- Feel good emotionally (less hurt)
- Hide my inadequacies to feel safe
- Pay back or get revenge

I Can Affect or Control You
- Cause embarrassment/pain
- Create indebtedness to me
- Stir up trouble or provoke
- Create codependency
- Manipulate or exploit
- Wield power

God Reigns
- Be a good steward of what I have
- Be in relationship with Jesus
- Care for God's Temple—my body
- Enlist prayer warriors
- Give glory to God
- Love as Jesus first loved me
- Obey the Ruler of the universe
- Spread good news of the gospel
- Use my gifts for the kingdom
- Become more Christ-like
- Be righteous (do what's right)
- Discover truth/wisdom
- Follow God's plan for my life
- Have Christ-like relationships
- Mature in my faith
- Represent Jesus to someone
- Take care of those entrusted to me
- Work as if working for the Lord

I Like to Investigate and Learn
- Experiment/discover/research
- Offer a new opinion/method
- Master a new skill
- Satisfy curiosity

I Want It, Need It, or Deserve It
- Get rich
- Go wherever I want
- I'm exempt from the rules
- Get what I've worked for/paid for
- Have nice things/satisfy desires
- I'm entitled to better treatment

I Respect People and Our Planet
- Make a difference
- Offer hope/love/gratitude
- Reduce suffering/meet a need
- Offer comic relief
- Open lines of communication
- Show respect/give honor

Other Motive: _____

Further Instructions: Scan the chart to find your top three Primary Motive Groupings—those groups with the most lines drawn toward them. List them here in priority order by total number of lines drawn. (**P**arent-**T**eenager)

P Top Motive Box _____ # of lines _____

T Top Motive Box _____ # of lines _____

P Second Motive Box _____ # of lines _____

T Second Motive Box _____ # of lines _____

P Third Motive Box _____ # of lines _____

T Third Motive Box _____ # of lines _____

Reflection Questions about your motives:

1. Which are your top three *Primary Motive Groupings* for positive and negative actions? In what way does this surprise or encourage you?

2. Regarding the action *Discover my life purpose*, what motive did you select and why?

3. Did any of your actions point toward this box: *I Respect People and Our Planet*? This motive (reason) is triggered by one's heartfelt desire to be a good human being, to do what's right for the sake of other human beings. It's often referred to as humanism, meaning the action is not necessarily done out of love for Jesus, but rather out of love or concern for others. If you marked anything in this category, talk about which of those answers might also have a *God Reigns* motive.

Individuals impact your life in a positive or negative manner. God has wired you to enjoy relationships that help you grow spiritually, develop Christ-like character, and complete the trustworthy task to which you've been commissioned. You're expected to weed out the poor relationships that are hindering your life mission—putting it in harm's way—and damaging your credibility as God's representative.

This exercise will allow you to think through your relationships—including your best friend, boss, spouse, coach, grandfather, neighbor, tutor, and others—in light of God's call on your life.

Exercise #2: My Relationships

Instructions: Without naming names, use this coding system to think about how each of your relationships has been enhancing or attempting to sabotage God's plan—or has not been doing anything at all.

- A Blessing to Me = **+**

- A Negative Influence on Me = **−**

- Neutral; No Dramatic Effect on Me = **N**

Limit your focus in certain categories, like "Neighbor," to the one individual in that grouping who has been the most influential—whether to the positive or negative side. If a particular relationship doesn't exist in your life, leave the code blank. *Don't try to guess your teenager's answers!*

Relationship	Parent	Teenager
Best Friend		
Boss		
Boyfriend or Girlfriend		
Brother/Stepbrother		
Church Member		
Coach		
Counselor/Therapist		
Cousin, Nephew, or Niece		
Coworker		
Father/Stepfather		
Grandfather		
Grandmother		
Ministry Partner		
Mother/Stepmother		
Neighbor		
Other Friend		
Pastor		

Prayer/Accountability Partner		
Role Model or Hero		
Sister/Stepsister		
Teacher		
Tutor or Mentor		
Uncle or Aunt		
Youth Leader		

Further Instructions: Count up the total number of each code (+ – N) on the chart and write that number below to find out whether you have more positive, negative, or neutral relationships.

Parent: + _____   Teenager: + _____

Parent: – _____   Teenager: – _____

Parent: **N** _____   Teenager: **N** _____

Reflection Questions about your relationships:

1. What number of positive, negative, and neutral relationships do you have? In what way does this surprise, encourage, or concern you?

2. Which negative relationship might you want to rethink because it's stunting your spiritual growth or the character formation you need for your life mission?

Note: Remember that I'm the first to applaud parenting as an ordained life mission that is a huge part of the legacy you will leave. For this exercise, though, we are targeting your most unique life assignment, without negating your daily duties.

Your calendar reflects your priorities—your most important daily commitments. Is your use of time driving you to leave a legacy? Do you make time to sit with God to hear about the bigger picture of your destiny? Remember that 12-year-old Jesus, who stayed behind at the temple to do kingdom work, said, *"Did you not know that I must be about My Father's business?" (Luke 2:49 NKJV).* Does your use of time reflect that you, too, are about God's business of redeeming the world?

Your 24/7 Time Clock Categories:

Chores	Church Services	Cooking/Eating	**Entertainment**
Exercise	Family Care	**Friends**	**Hobbies**
Homework	Job	Ministry	**Organizations**
Quiet Time	School	**Shopping**	Sleeping
Spiritual Growth	**Sports**	**Style/Grooming**	Volunteer Work

Imagine that you were asked to go on a life-changing search to find 12 minutes per day to redirect toward fulfilling God's call on your life—toward your most bold, distinct, and far-reaching life purpose. In reality, this is no silly scavenger hunt to find minutes; this is a serious step in reprioritizing your time to accomplish what will outlast you. Do you think you could find 12 minutes in your current 24-hour day to use solely to focus on your life mission?

Exercise #3: My Use of Time

Instructions: Your challenge is to pull 12 minutes from the seven **highlighted** Time Clock Categories only—areas that may offer you more flexibility each day to focus on your most unique life purpose. *Don't try to guess your teenager's answers!* (**P**arent-**T**eenager)

12-Minutes-Per-Day Challenge
Finding 2-4-6 Minutes to Focus on God's Call on My Life

- To pray specifically about my most unique life purpose, I'll grab 2 minutes from...

  P _____

  T _____

- To brainstorm with others about that life purpose, I'll grab 4 minutes from...

  P _____

  T _____

- To work on specific life mission tasks, I'll grab 6 minutes from...

  P _____

  T _____

Reflection Questions about your use of time:

1. Share your logic and feelings about having moved some time around.

2. After you read this book, do you think you'll actually incorporate this reassignment of time into your daily schedule—even if all the time is spent in prayer and brainstorming for now? Explain your thoughts.

Will You?

What if your dearest friend—someone who cared deeply about helping you remove the roadblocks that are delaying the discovery and fulfillment of your unique life mission—offered you excellent advice about your motives, relationships, and use of time? Would you heed your friend's advice? Likewise, will you, in preparation for your boldest assignment, lean into the insight you've prayerfully gained from these exercises? What is one definitive step you can take immediately in this area that will impact your day-to-day living and (if you have a glimpse of it already) your unique life mission?

To wrap up your parent-teenager conversation with intentionality:

- **Encourage your teenager to summarize his insights, by asking a question like this:** *Starting now, how will your insight about your motives, relationships, and use of time affect your day-to-day living and (if you have a glimpse of it already) your unique life mission?*

- **Challenge your teenager and yourself to memorize the verse at the beginning of this chapter.**

- **Affirm with a positive statement about who your teenager is in Christ.**

- **Close by personalizing a brief prayer, like this:**

  God, thank you that you've gently shown us the importance of rethinking our motives, relationships, and use of our time. We pray these exercises brought honor to you, as we learned to focus on topics that will help us complete our perfectly-wired-in life mission. We ask for your continued guidance. In Jesus' name we pray. Amen.

  Also, keep praying that the Holy Spirit will reveal your life verse. Tell your teenager (and vice versa), if you think you've found it!

CHAPTER 7

KNOWING YOUR STRENGTHS, WEAKNESSES, OPPORTUNITIES, AND THREATS

And I am certain that God, who began the good work within you, will continue his work until it is finally finished on the day when Christ Jesus returns (Philippians 1:6).

Helmet Head

In my teenage years, acne could have signed a death warrant to my self-esteem, but I rebounded because I had the good sense to play up one great asset: my girly blonde locks. So, when I was able to style a perfect hairdo for the day, I couldn't risk losing that fabulous coif in the wind or commotion of life. Duty called me to lacquer on three layers of hairspray to cement every hair in its flawless place, thus preserving my self-confidence.

I'm telling you that a hug with a head-bump from me could've knocked you out! I was even called "helmet head," but did I care? No, my *spot-on* hairstyle was my opportunity to rock it.

God doesn't expect you and your teenager to have everything in your lives cemented down into cast iron perfection. Instead, you're expected to know your strengths, weaknesses, opportunities, and threats—so you can play up the good stuff and minimize the not-so-good stuff. Doing this will help you both shine for Jesus with long-term significance and purpose.

This chapter should come with some type of reward coupon for a back and neck massage. It isn't an easy set of concepts to wrestle to the ground—it could wear you out and give you a royal pain in the neck! We're addressing a strategy for how you can cooperate with God to discover the life you were intended to live: **Knowing Your Strengths, Weaknesses, Opportunities, and Threats**. This best practice will reveal who you really are. (After you work through the materials, you can invite your teenager to discuss these topics with you.)

Tip about how to cooperate with God's plan: If I know myself well— my strengths, weaknesses, opportunities, and threats—God's "This I Must Do" purpose for my life will become clearer and more doable. (And the same is true for your teenager!)

How to Have a Conversation With Your Teenager

After you've completed all four exercises in this chapter, follow these guidelines:

1. On the "Strengths" and "Opportunities" exercises, you have the option of using light, tentative pencil markings to indicate how you think your teenager might answer. However, for the "Weaknesses" and "Threats" exercises, the instructions will indicate that you're not to try to guess your teenager's answers.

2. As you hand off this book to your teenager, encourage her to read the opening remarks of the chapter and the topical explanations that are prior to the exercises. Or you can offer to give a brief overview of this chapter's topics and to answer any related questions.

3. Ask your teenager to use red or blue ink to do the four exercises, leaving any incorrect pencil notations—for a fun, lively comparison.

4. When it's time to kick off your parent-teenager conversation, open your time by personalizing a brief prayer, like this:

    Holy Spirit, give us ears to hear what's really being said, along with insightful and kind words to use during this conversation about our SWOT analysis. We invite you to join us and give us wisdom beyond our years. This we pray. Amen.

5. Discuss the Reflection Questions for all four exercises, treasuring the God-centered time with your teenager.

Note: Give grace abundantly to your teenager and yourself. In fact, pour it on lavishly!

SWOT

SWOT doesn't mean Special Weapons And Tactics team, like police departments use in hostage situations. That's S-W-A-T and this is S-W-O-T. The SWOT we're talking about is a strategic planning method that stands for Strengths, Weaknesses, Opportunities, and Threats.

Companies use a SWOT analysis to take stock of their assets (good stuff like their great customer service) and also their liabilities (stuff that might harm their business, like not having enough cash to stay afloat). They're trying to identify the things that will help them reach their goals or cause them to miss the mark.

I'm really grateful to the very smart business consultant who invented this process (strategic planner Albert Humphrey), because we as Christians can use the same formula to call to mind all those strengths and opportunities that can enhance God's strategic plan for our lives, along with all the weaknesses and threats that can sabotage it.

Let's look at one letter of SWOT at a time to see how this process works.

Know My Strengths

(Natural Talents, Résumé Skills, and Learned Abilities)

God wired you with all your cool strengths at birth and helped you develop other great ones along the way. Your strengths (natural talents, résumé skills, and learned abilities) are cause for daily celebration, and they'll help launch your life's work.

Even if you're having one of those days when you don't feel like you're good at anything, allow God to give you insight into your uniqueness.

Exercise #1: My Strengths

Instructions: Check all the strengths that apply to you, or write your answer. (□ **P**arent □ **T**eenager)

Strengths

P	T		P	T	
□	□	Act/Perform/Entertain	□	□	Build/Repair/Remodel
□	□	Care for Animals	□	□	Compete in Sports
□	□	Cook/Garden	□	□	Crunch Numbers/Formulas
□	□	Dance	□	□	Design/Fashion/Graphics
□	□	Drive	□	□	Lead/Manage
□	□	Manage Public Relations	□	□	Marketing
□	□	Mentor/Counsel/Coach	□	□	Organize/Plan/Create
□	□	Paint/Draw/Photograph	□	□	Perform Medical Procedures
□	□	Program Computers	□	□	Protect/Rescue/Represent
□	□	Research/Invent	□	□	Sales
□	□	Sing/Play an Instrument	□	□	Speak Multiple Languages/Sign
□	□	Speak/Teach/Host	□	□	Style/Hair/Makeup/Clothes
□	□	Supervise/Babysit	□	□	Unearth/Reconstruct/Restore
□	□	Technology	□	□	Volunteer/Serve
□	□	Write	□	□	Other:

Reflection Questions about your strengths:

1. Which top two or three natural talents, résumé skills, or learned abilities has God given you or helped you develop?

2. Do you like the strengths you have, or would you rather God give you some different ones? Explain. If you'd prefer new ones, which ones—and why?

3. How have you used any of your strengths to do God's work on earth—or how could you use them when the season is right?

Know My Weaknesses

You're not alone in having weaknesses. We live in a fallen world that confuses us constantly about how we should react to life's pressures and temptations. We're all sinners doing our best with God's help, hoping that we don't get thrown off course any more than we already have, as we follow the pathway to purpose.

What would you consider your most pressing weaknesses right now—things that might be blocking you from all that God is calling you to be or do? Don't be shy about admitting them. Nobody skates through life without faults. Ask yourself, "How does God want to transform me? Is there something I can do to cooperate with God that will actually prepare me well for my life mission?"

Exercise #2: My Weaknesses

Instructions: Check or write one or two personal weaknesses that you feel comfortable noting. *Don't try to guess your teenager's answers!* (□ **P**arent □ **T**eenager)

Weaknesses

P	T		P	T	
□	□	Aggression/Temper	□	□	Bitterness/Regret
□	□	Codependency	□	□	Controlling Nature
□	□	Fear	□	□	Impatience
□	□	Insecurity/Self-Criticism	□	□	Instant Gratification
□	□	Intolerance	□	□	Irresponsibility/Laziness
□	□	Jealousy	□	□	Judgmental Tone
□	□	Lying/Lack of Integrity	□	□	Overcommitment
□	□	Over-Emotionalism	□	□	Over-Indulgence/Greed
□	□	Perfectionism	□	□	Pride/Self-Centeredness
□	□	Procrastination	□	□	Quitter Attitude
□	□	Sense of Entitlement	□	□	Undisciplined Mouth
□	□	Unfairness	□	□	Ungrateful Heart
□	□	Wastefulness	□	□	Other:

Reflection Questions about your weaknesses:

1. What's one of your weaknesses? If you'd like, give a few details about how it has affected your life.

2. Close your eyes and point to any weakness on the chart. How could that weakness block a person's readiness and ability to serve God wholeheartedly?

3. In your opinion, which two of the weaknesses on the chart are the ugliest, cruelest, or saddest? Explain why—being extra careful not to name names or gossip about those you know who have this weakness.

Let's move on to something a little more cheerful: opportunities, or what some might call *lucky breaks* and Christians know can be *God's favor*. Our lives are filled with opportunities that allow us to get a front-row seat to watch our distinctive purpose unfold before our very eyes. Stay alert for opportunities that God might be sending you to explore the fascination in your soul or to fulfill your deepest longing.

One quick warning here: Not every opportunity is God's will for you at a particular time, so it's important to weigh all of them prayerfully.

What would you consider your biggest opportunities right now (or in the foreseeable future) to helping you accomplish all that God is calling you to be and do? Look at these options as if they were God's gift to you—because they might be. Sort through them for inspiration that could change the course of your life.

Exercise #3: My Opportunities

Instructions: Check all the opportunities that apply to you, or write your answer. (□ **P**arent □ **T**eenager)

Opportunities

To explore jobs that relate to my life purpose:

P T

□ □ Apply for an internship or paid position to learn skills related to my life purpose.

□ □ Interview a Christian business mentor about God's call on my life.

□ □ Take a college or seminary class that offers coursework in my area of passion.

□ □ Other:

To explore my life mission:

P T

□ □ Experiment with a leadership role—in any healthy area—just to practice leading.

□ □ "Go fishing" in the ministry pool to see if I might like a brand-new ministry.

□ □ Sign up for a mission trip—near or far—to broaden my perspective.

□ □ Invite a support team to pray for my life mission.

□ □ Offer to serve at a community event that piques my interest.

□ □ Other:

To start a specific ministry:

P T

□ □ Begin a local ministry for children who have a parent in jail.

□ □ Collect shoes or jackets for the poor.

□ □ Start a mentoring program for pregnant teenagers.

□ □ Volunteer to work with drug-addicted infants.

□ □ Start an intercessory prayer team at my church.

□ □ Other:

To grow spiritually:

P   T

☐   ☐   Practice a spiritual habit, like tithing, fasting, or living a simpler lifestyle.

☐   ☐   Create an accountability friendship with someone I admire and respect.

☐   ☐   Get counseling regarding my grief, relationships, abuse, or addiction.

☐   ☐   Keep a spiritual journal of miracles in my life.

☐   ☐   Pray for a God-honoring dating relationship.

☐   ☐   Seek a spiritual mentor to help me see my sufficiency in Christ.

☐   ☐   Spend more time in God's Word to develop a deeper relationship with Jesus.

☐   ☐   Stop my endless mind chatter and the extra noise that drown out God's voice.

☐   ☐   Other:

Reflection Questions about your opportunities:

1. What one or two opportunities do you have in your life right now or have you had in the past? In what way might at least one of them be related to your life's most unique contribution?

2. How would you feel about a God-manufactured opportunity coming true to do what you love doing in ministry? What would be the ideal scenario?

Know My Threats

You can count on the fact that numerous troubles will crop up to threaten your life mission. External threats sneak up on you to leave you exhausted, irritable, overcommitted, frustrated, embarrassed, fearful, angry, sad, with low self-esteem, or facing consequences. These threats are real, and they can rob you of God's best design for your life if you don't take measures to eliminate them.

What would you consider your biggest threats to being and doing all that God is calling you to be and do? It's a given that Satan puts a target on the backs of those who are doing the will of God. My prayer for you comes from 2 Corinthians 1:10 (NIV)—*He has delivered us from such a deadly peril [threats], and he will deliver us again. On him we have set our hope that he will continue to deliver us.*

Exercise #4: My Threats

Instructions: Check or write one or two personal weaknesses—that you feel comfortable noting. *Don't try to guess your teenager's answers.*
(□ **P**arent □ **T**eenager)

Threats

P	T		P	T	
□	□	Abuse	□	□	Credit Card Debt/Gambling
□	□	Depression	□	□	Disorganization/Clutter
□	□	Drama-Drama-Drama	□	□	Dysfunctional/Broken Home
□	□	Excessive TV/Gaming/Internet/Phone	□	□	Friend Who's a Bad Influence
□	□	Illness/Disability	□	□	Issues About Body Image
□	□	Junk Food/Excessive Eating	□	□	Lack of Funding for My Dreams
□	□	No Accountability/Prayer Partners	□	□	No Gym/Exercise Routine
□	□	Obsessive E-mails/Tweets/Texts/Posts	□	□	Parties With Irresistible Temptations
□	□	Pornographic Images	□	□	Shopping Malls/eBay®/TV Offers
□	□	Someone Else's Agenda for My Life	□	□	Tobacco/Alcohol/Drugs/Prescriptions
□	□	Violent Movies/Trashy Novels	□	□	Other:

Reflection Questions about threats to eliminate from your life:

1. What's one threat you're facing? If you'd like, give a few details about how it has affected your life.

2. Close your eyes and point to any threat on the chart. How could that threat sabotage God's finest plans for a person?

3. What do you feel is the worst threat a person can face? Explain why—being extra careful not to name names or gossip about those you know who face this threat.

Do you know yourself well enough to suspect your next, logical steps regarding your strengths, weaknesses, opportunities, and threats? If you had more than a suspicion about how this logic would ignite your life mission, would you take those steps? Will you, in preparation for a magnificent assignment to come, move forward now in at least one such area of your life? In what way will your prayerful insight about your SWOT analysis specifically and immediately affect your day-to-day living and (if you have a glimpse of it already) your unique life mission?

To wrap up your parent-teenager conversation with intentionality:

- **Encourage your teenager to summarize his insights, by asking a question like this:** *Starting now, how will your insight from your SWOT analysis affect your day-to-day living and (if you have a glimpse of it already) your unique life mission?*

- **Challenge your teenager and yourself to memorize the verse at the beginning of this chapter.**

- **Affirm with a positive statement about who your teenager is in Christ.**

- **Close by personalizing a brief prayer, like this:**

  God, please bless us for our willingness to take a hard look at ourselves in this SWOT analysis. Thank you for all the strengths and opportunities you've wired into our lives. We ask you to turn our weaknesses into strengths—and to protect us from all that threatens our life mission. In Jesus' name we pray. Amen.

  Also, keep praying that the Holy Spirit will reveal your life verse. Tell your teenager (and vice versa), if you think you've found it!

CHAPTER 8

PRAYING FOR COURAGE, PERSEVERANCE, AND MIRACLES

"This is my command—be strong and courageous! Do not be afraid or discouraged. For the Lord your God is with you wherever you go"
(Joshua 1:9).

Lion Mauls Anne Hjelle

Anne was a 32-year-old petite, 5-foot-4 blonde I hired to be my personal athletic trainer for a season. She was a great inspiration to me, physically, mentally, and spiritually. You see, a few years earlier, on January 8, 2004, she'd been mauled by a 122-pound mountain lion at Whiting Ranch Wilderness Park in Southern California while mountain biking down a bumpy trail. Normally, the oak woodland park is paradise for hikers, mountain bikers, and equestrians, but just prior to Anne's attack, that same mountain lion had killed and partially devoured another rider, Mark Reynolds, 35, on the same trail.

During Anne's ordeal, she persistently prayed, "Jesus, help me!"—relying on the full power of her Christian faith. (Feel free to skip to the last sentence of this paragraph to avoid graphic details.) The cougar chomped down hard on her head and face, trying to drag her off the trail. The animal's fangs even punctured her neck, missing critical arteries by millimeters. Her riding partner, Debi Nicholls, began a courageous tug-of-war with the beast—with Anne as the rope—and was finally able to free her friend from the mountain lion's jaws. Surgeons performed five operations with more than 200 stitches to complete the miracle of one of the greatest-ever escapes.

When the humble and grateful-to-be-alive Anne speaks to groups now (public speaking is her new worst fear), she says that fear isn't really our biggest problem. It's our reaction to the fear that matters. She emphasizes that God doesn't want us to live in fear. What great advice for your teenager and you to consider as you bolt down the pathway to purpose into the unknown to discover and fulfill God's unique plan for your lives. Pray for the courage, perseverance, and miracles you'll need, even when fear pounces on you like a hungry mountain lion—which it will.

Best Practice #4

God assigned a unique purpose to you before the world began. And you can rest assured that this proven practice—**Praying for Courage, Perseverance, and Miracles**—is a primary method of hearing the details of that plan! When you sit quietly to pray simple, bold, and specific prayers and then listen for answers, God can reveal the best-possible method for you to accomplish your life mission. (After you work through the materials, you can invite your teenager to discuss these topics with you.)

Tip about how to cooperate with God's plan: If I pray for courage, perseverance, and miracles to help me accomplish my life mission, I'll receive those gifts from God. (And the same is true for your teenager!)

How to Have a Conversation With Your Teenager

After you've completed all three exercises in this chapter, follow these guidelines:

1. On the "Courage" exercise, you have the option of using light, tentative pencil markings to indicate how you think your teenager might answer. However, for the "Perseverance" and "Miracles" exercises, the instructions will indicate that you're not to try to guess your teenager's answers. That's only because they're sentence-format answers that would have to be erased.

2. As you hand off this book to your teenager, encourage her to read the opening remarks of the chapter and the topical explanations that are prior to the exercises. Or you can offer to give a brief overview of this chapter's topics and to answer any related questions.

3. Ask your teenager to use red or blue ink to do the three exercises, leaving any incorrect pencil notations—for a fun, lively comparison.

4. When it's time to kick off your parent-teenager conversation, open your time by personalizing a brief prayer, like this:

    Holy Spirit, we ask you to continue to form a partnership between you and each of us, as well as a stronger partnership between us as parent-teenager. We also ask that you open our eyes to the truth about how courage, perseverance, and miracles affect our ability to follow your lead in launching our life missions. This we pray. Amen.

5. Discuss the Reflection Questions for all three exercises, treasuring the God-centered time with your teenager.

Note: Fear can be overwhelming, so be extra patient and kind while discussing this topic with your teenager.

Pray for Courage

Courage is not the absence of fear but the ability to withstand fear. It's the strength to take risks, face danger, or endure trials. It's often difficult to find courage, so remember that God loves you, wired you with courage, and wants to answer your prayers to outsmart your fears or remove them. Let fear motivate you to seek God's power.

Jesus commands us to be fearless. That's not to say that God won't use you in a mighty way if you're afraid. Brace yourself to be used, even if fear is your middle name. Esther, for example, was terribly afraid to risk dying—which was the penalty for approaching the king uninvited. Esther 4:16 tells us that, eventually, she said, *"If I must die, I must die."* That means she moved forward in spite of her fears.

But before we get too focused on the type of Esther-courage of which heroes are made, we'd better look at the basic courage that's needed to overcome everyday obstacles in your life. Do you have any commonplace fears, like these?

- Flying

- Spiders

- Public speaking

- Terrorism

These types of daily fears, if they get out of control, can lock you in a nightmarish prison. They may lead to health issues, like sleep disorders and high blood pressure. They may cause psychological problems, like depression, phobias, paranoia, and hypochondria. They may create emotional stress—the stress of worry, nervousness, and even lying. They may rob you of opportunities to bless others and for God to bless you. And they may block the creativity, productivity, and relationships you need for your life mission.

To fulfill the larger-than-life legacy that's been gifted to you, you need to be brave enough to pull off some tough assignments—but you won't be able to do that without asking for God's courage. It's time now, during this critical season of your life, to learn to use bold prayers for courage to increase your faith. You do this by setting aside time to focus on God's strength and to ask for the courage you need to proceed in the direction of your destiny.

Taking courage happens when you recognize that God is faithful and will help you. And if you remember God's unshakable love for you in the past, you'll be assured of God's faithfulness today and tomorrow. Don't let fear sidetrack you from your life's calling.

Just like Peter in Matthew 14, you are called to step out of the boat and walk on water. But that huge step requires believing that Jesus will catch you when you start to sink under the terrifying waves of life. Would you like to quit running and hiding from your deepest daily fears? Are you willing to give God the fears you have about living out your daring, risk-filled purpose? If so, now is a good time to take courage.

Exercise #1: My Courage

Instructions: Check all the fears you've ever had—or write your answer. Then write your five biggest, current fears in priority order, high to low. (□ **Parent** □ **Teenager**)

Common Fears

P	T		P	T	
□	□	Bridges	□	□	Bullies
□	□	Cancer/MS/Diabetes	□	□	Claustrophobia
□	□	Conflict/Harsh Words	□	□	Consequences
□	□	Darkness	□	□	Desertion/Abandonment
□	□	Disability	□	□	Divorce/Separation
□	□	Doctors/Dentists	□	□	Dogs/Snakes/Spiders
□	□	Dying/Death	□	□	Embarrassment
□	□	Failure	□	□	Flying
□	□	Foreclosure/Bankruptcy	□	□	Global Warming
□	□	Going to Jail	□	□	Heart Attack/Surgery
□	□	Heights	□	□	HIV-Positive Contact
□	□	Hunger/Homelessness	□	□	Illness of Loved One
□	□	"Jesus Freak" Label	□	□	Injury by Attack/Car Accident
□	□	Kidnappers/Sex Traffic Rings	□	□	Lack of Ministry Funds
□	□	Loneliness	□	□	Losing My Ministry
□	□	Moral Failure	□	□	Natural Disaster (flood, quake)
□	□	Online Predators/Scam Artists	□	□	Panic Attack
□	□	Poor Job Performance	□	□	Poor Reputation
□	□	Poverty	□	□	Public Speaking
□	□	Purposelessness	□	□	Rejection/Criticism
□	□	Repenting of Pet Sin	□	□	Ridicule About Appearance
□	□	Scary Life Mission	□	□	Secret Being Found Out
□	□	Sharing the Gospel	□	□	Sin Being Exposed
□	□	Small Group Dynamics	□	□	Social Phobia/Anxiety
□	□	Starting Over in Life	□	□	Strangers

☐	☐	Success	☐	☐	Surrendering to Jesus
☐	☐	Swimming/Drowning	☐	☐	Telling the Truth
☐	☐	Terrorism/Bombs	☐	☐	Unemployment
☐	☐	Other:			

Top 5 Fears (1=High, 5=Low)

Parent	Teenager
1. _____	1. _____
2. _____	2. _____
3. _____	3. _____
4. _____	4. _____
5. _____	5. _____

Reflection Questions about your fears:

1. How many fears did you check or write? Did that number surprise you? Why or why not?

2. What are your top two fears? Share a few details.

3. In what way does one of your fears interfere with God's call on your life?

4. How does fear keep you focused on yourself?

Instructions: Check the box that indicates the type of courage you most need to continue becoming all God wants you to be.
(□ Parent □ Teenager)

Three Types of Courage

P T

□ □ **Courage to Step In:** Help someone who's struggling or afraid; befriend someone who's different from the norm; start a ministry; rally others to help

□ □ **Courage to Step Out:** Face a criticism, illness, situation, or psychological fear; make a personal or relational change; stretch myself; be myself; take a risk; try something new

□ □ **Courage to Step Up:** Fight against evil or injustice; confront a wrong; tell the truth; stand up for myself; join a cause; defend my beliefs; lobby for change

Reflection Question about your courage:

- Which type of courage do you feel you most need to develop, and why?

Write and pray aloud a simple, bold, and specific Prayer for Courage:

P: *God, take this fear from me:* _____

_____

I trust you to give me your courage. Thank you in advance!

T: *God, take this fear from me:* _____

_____

I trust you to give me your courage. Thank you in advance!

Next, let's look at Perseverance and Miracles at the same time, because they're closely connected to one another—and to the concept of Courage, too, that we just talked about!

Satan's strategy is very simple: To keep you from persevering and expecting miracles, he steals your courage to make you afraid. He knows that fear will cause you to give up and doubt God's best—when progress seems impossible. Your mind will wage war against your emotions, saying: *I can't go on—Yes I can—No I can't—Yes I can!*

The typical dictionary synonyms for the word *perseverance* are *persistence, endurance,* and *pressing on.* So, let me ask you: In your daily life, not your Big Dream life, but your everyday, ordinary life—do you persist? Do you have stick-to-itiveness? Do you complete projects like remodeling your kitchen or balancing the budget? Do you follow through on community commitments, even if you don't feel like it? This is great practice for your life mission. It's like a dress rehearsal for what you were created to do. It's nothing less than God's training ground for bigger assignments to come.

You see, when God gives you a behemoth dream, it'll take every ounce of your fortitude, persistence, due diligence, and faith in supernatural miracles to complete the task. Yes, the job will seem too big, and there will always be somebody who'll try to discourage you. If you stay the course, though, and have patience until the end, you'll reap great rewards—the biggest of which is the joy of knowing that you completed the task you were called by God to do!

You must cover your dream with simple prayers for perseverance and miracles by asking, boldly and specifically, for the help you need—all the while recalling God's miracles for you in the past. It's the recollection of past miracles in your life, when you experienced God's unshakable love, that will breathe hope into you for future miracles when the going gets tough. And I guarantee you, the going will get tough!

God has assigned to you a unique purpose for your life, for which commitment is a basic trait you'll need. When you develop your character to persevere to the end and to hope against all odds for miracles, you're declaring: "There's no turning back from what God called me to do! I won't quit until I complete my mission in life." Are you ready to make a commitment to finish what God is calling you to do?

Exercise #2: My Perseverance

Instructions: Write a brief answer to the following questions. *Don't try to guess your teenager's answers!* (**P**arent-**T**eenager)

When I Persevered to the End: Describe your stick-to-itiveness in an important task or difficult situation. Mention your earthly reward for not giving up.

P _____

_____

T _____

_____

Daily Life: Name one area in which you need to persevere now.

P _____

_____

T _____

_____

Bigger-Than-Life Assignment: Name one area in which you must persevere to accomplish God's will for your life long-term.

P _____

_____

T _____

_____

Reflection Questions about your past, present, and future perseverance:

1. In what way did you benefit from persevering in a certain situation?

2. Are you willing to persevere in your bigger-than-life assignment, even though some of the details are still foggy? Why?

Write and pray aloud a simple, bold, and specific Prayer for Perseverance:

P: *God, I believe you want me to persevere in this situation:* _____ _____.

I trust you to help me, even though I feel like giving up. Thank you in advance!

T: *God, I believe you want me to persevere in this situation:* _____ _____.

I trust you to help me, even though I feel like giving up. Thank you in advance!

Exercise #3: My Miracles

- The greatest miracle of our lives: That God chose us and uses us in spite of our sinfulness.

- The most commonly overlooked miracle today: Answered prayer!

- Other miracles in our lives: Childbirth, Clothing, Education, Faith, Family, Financial Blessings, Food, Forgiveness, Freedom, Friends, God's Presence, Healing, Health, Hope, Job, Love, Ministry, Nature's Beauty, Peace Amidst Trials, Safety, Second Chance, Shelter, Spiritual Growth, Strength, Transportation, Victory

Instructions: Write a brief answer to the following questions. *Don't try to guess your teenager's answers!* (**P**arent-**T**eenager)

Remembering My Favorite Miracle: Ask God to help you recall some of the numerous miracles in your life and the lives of your loved ones. Write your favorite miracle, giving a few details.

P _____

_____

T _____

_____

Daily Life: What next miracle would you like to see God perform immediately?

P _____

_____

T _____

_____

Bigger-Than-Life Assignment: What miracle do you need to happen to live out God's boldest dream for your life?

P _____

_____

T _____

_____

Reflection Questions about the miracles you've seen and still need:

1. What are a few details of your favorite-ever miracle? Why is it your favorite?

2. Why is there no limit to God's potential miracles in your life?

3. Are you willing to pray for a miracle in your bigger-than-life assignment, even though some of the details are still foggy? Why?

Write and pray aloud a simple, bold, and specific Prayer for a Miracle:

P: *God, I need you to perform a miracle for me in this situation:* _____

_____

I trust you to use your mighty power. Thank you in advance!

T: *God, I need you to perform a miracle for me in this situation:* _____

_____

I trust you to use your mighty power. Thank you in advance!

When you lose your courage and feel like quitting a task and giving up all expectations for a miracle to happen, that's the time to remember these truths:

- Quitters run away in fear when they get *discouraged*, but you turn to God who's faithful to help you stand with *courage*.

- Quitters put themselves down, but you're able to *persevere in faith* when you remember who you are in Christ.

- Quitters exaggerate their problems and worry about everything, but you expect God's never-ending *miraculous interventions*.

- Quitters become exhausted, but you rest in the Lord and seek nourishment for the long haul *through confident prayer*.

God will provide all you need—as far as courage, perseverance, and miracles—to accomplish his will and purpose.

What if you were awarded one do-over in your life regarding:

- Taking courage against a fear

- Persisting on an important task

- Expecting a miracle

Which do-over from your life would you choose? The good news is that you really don't have to choose. You can have a second chance, starting right now, in all three areas by laying your heart before God and asking for courage, perseverance, and miracles to abound in your daily life and for your long-term, kingdom goals. Will you, in preparation for a God-designed assignment, move forward now in at least one such area of your life by praying simple, bold, and specific prayers for what you need? In what way will your prayerful insight in this area now directly affect your day-to-day living and (if you have a glimpse of it already) your unique life mission?

To wrap up your parent-teenager conversation with intentionality:

- **Encourage your teenager to summarize her insights, by asking a question like this:** *Starting now, how will your insight about courage, perseverance, and miracles affect your day-to-day living and (if you have a glimpse of it already) your unique life mission?*

- **Challenge your teenager and yourself to memorize the verse at the beginning of this chapter.**

- **Affirm with a positive statement about who your teenager is in Christ.**

- **Close by personalizing a brief prayer, like this:**

  God, help us be strong and courageous, rather than discouraged and afraid. Go with us wherever you send us, so we'll have the courage to

persevere to the end of the boldest task for which we've been wired—
expecting miracles every step of the way. In Jesus' name we pray.
Amen.

Also, keep praying that the Holy Spirit will reveal your life verse.
Tell your teenager (and vice versa) if you think you've found it!

CHAPTER 9

WRITING YOUR LIFETIME DREAM STATEMENT

Many are the plans in a human heart, but it is the Lord's purpose that prevails (Proverbs 19:21 TNIV).

Mother Teresa's Pure Joy

In 1988, my 67-year-old mother and I, who both loved Jesus dearly, stuffed two backpacks with the bare essentials of life and flew to Calcutta, India—each of us for a different, specific purpose. My mom wanted and actually expected to meet Mother Teresa, her heroine, even though I kept warning her that the odds of that happening were nil to zero.

Personally, I wanted to ask the Missionaries of Charity, who ministered there with Mother Teresa, how they could work with the poorest of the poor in a city of 11 million people, including 60,000 homeless. I figured that if the nuns could explain to me why they had such passion about an apparently disheartening life mission, perhaps it would then be a cakewalk for me to understand how to find a somewhat lovelier life mission in a much more sanitized environment! I was desperate for answers.

Upon arriving in Calcutta, my mom and I saw dilapidated shacks made of bamboo, paper, plastic, mud, cardboard, and tires. The women were making cow dung patties in the fields to use as cooking fuel beneath their makeshift hotplates. We saw children relieving themselves in the gutters and others using the same gutter water for bathing and washing dishes.

To my utter amazement, when the Mother House front door flung open, a young, sari-clad novice (nun-in-training) immediately ushered us upstairs to meet the barefoot Mother Teresa. Still stunned, I couldn't even take in the fact that Mother Teresa was actually bowing to us and inviting us to sit with her on an old wooden bench. My mom gave me her famous *I told you so* grin and helped carry the conversation, until I could do a quick reality check to bring myself out of shock. I remember thinking, *Katie, this really is happening right now. Get a grip and ask the question you came to ask!* Abruptly, I heard myself nearly yelling into that Nobel Peace laureate's ear, "How can you do this work in these terrible slum conditions?"

A smile slowly spread across Mother Teresa's face and twinkled in her eyes, as she gently patted my arm and said, "It's pure joy."

For 15 years back home, I struggled to figure out how working in the slums could be anybody's pure joy. Finally, I understood that pure joy doesn't emanate from God revealing the perfect, meticulously wired, grand life mission. It's not even about the enormous privilege of doing the difficult work we've been assigned. It isn't about some lovely "feel good" reward or heavenly kudos we get for saintly obedience. In fact, it has nothing to do with us or our performance or all!

Instead, to me, pure joy is…

> *Jesus' abundant, unconditional love that overflows our heart's capacity to contain it, thus, spilling into those we're called to serve.*

I'm convinced that was the pure joy in Mother Teresa's heart. It was the spilling over of "Jesus-love" that gave her excess love to pour out to others—wherever, whenever, and however God called. First John 4:19 says it clearly: *We love each other because [God] loved us first.* That never-ending, all-filling, overflowing Jesus-love pours into us a gratitude and desire to surrender to God's plans, allowing us to complete our life mission humbly. It's why the greatest compliment you'll ever receive will be, "I can see Jesus in you. I want what you have! Tell me how to get it."

In Mother Teresa's case, her *overall, general, universal purpose in life* was, of course, to glorify God in all she did, using her *spiritual gift mix* of voluntary poverty, celibacy, leadership, compassion, and faith.

God had also designed her with a *specific passion* about the dignity of life and the relief of human suffering in the name of Jesus.

Her *unique life mission* (her lifetime dream—her pure-joy job!) was to deliver the life message, *"Jesus loves you,"* to the poorest of the poor, including refugees, ex-prostitutes, the mentally ill, abandoned children, lepers, AIDS victims, and the aged, sick, and dying.

Her *remarkable method of delivering her life message* (her vision of how to get her message out) was to do that work worldwide, opening centers and training and inspiring staff and volunteers who'd care for the disenfranchised of the world. Even after her death, her centers have continued to spread to more than 133 countries, with some 4,500 nuns, priests, and hundreds of thousands of lay workers.

That life mission is the *distinct, heart-pounding, far-reaching purpose* she'd been put on earth to fulfill. And her schoolteacher days—as a young, humble, dedicated nun—were the exact training ground she needed to prepare for her boldest work.

May Mother Teresa inspire you and your teenager to each take your own personal journey to purpose with your backpack fully loaded with Jesus-love. May that pure joy flow through you as you complete the God-orchestrated task that was yours before the world began—whether you're destined to serve in a sanitized environment or not!

So, you're really committed to living out the custom-made dream that God designed you to live, right? If so, you'll be blessed to invite God to reveal your emboldened purpose by using this best practice: **Writing Your Lifetime Dream Statement**. (After you work through the materials, you can invite your teenager to discuss this topic with you.)

A Lifetime Dream Statement is a God-inspired declaration that outlines your next steps on the pathway to purpose that will lead to the fulfillment of your dream. This brief statement (with four segments) will help you make the most far-reaching contribution of your life, one that could have ripple effects on countless people.

Tip about how to cooperate with God's plan: If I accept the unique life purpose that God designed specifically for me, I'll have a bold, passionate lifetime dream that far exceeds my highest hopes. (And the same is true for your teenager!)

How to Have a Conversation With Your Teenager

After you've completed all five exercises in this chapter, follow these guidelines:

1. For Exercises #1, 3, and 4, you have the option of using light, tentative pencil markings to indicate how you think your teenager might answer. However, for Exercises #2 and 5 about actually writing your life mission and your Lifetime Dream Statement, the instructions will indicate that you're not to try to guess your teenager's answers. That's only because they're sentence-format answers that would have to be erased.

2. As you hand off this book to your teenager, encourage him to read the opening remarks of the chapter and the topical explanations that are prior to the exercises. Or you can offer to give a brief overview of this chapter's topics and to answer any related questions.

3. Ask your teenager to use red or blue ink to do the five exercises, leaving any incorrect pencil notations—for a fun, lively comparison.

4. When it's time to kick off your parent-teenager conversation, open your time by personalizing a brief prayer, like this:

   Holy Spirit, the Bible tells us that a cord of three strands is not easily broken. Thank you for such a three-way partnership between you and us, as we have this conversation. Help us write and discuss our Lifetime Dream Statements about the bold purpose you've wired into each of our hearts. This we pray. Amen.

5. Discuss the Reflection Questions for all five exercises, treasuring the God-centered time with your teenager.

Note: Your teenager could fall easily into the trap of "I'm not good enough, holy enough, or smart enough to have a life mission that requires me to deliver a message to a group of people." If you sense this happening, remind your teenager that nobody is worthy enough, and that we're only made able through God's power!

Go ahead and ask God to reveal your lifetime dream in spite of your doubt, fears, and sins. The Bible tells us in Psalm 37:4, *Take delight in the Lord, and he will give you your heart's desires.*

This means that if you'll delight in the Lord, finding enormous joy in getting to know your Maker, then God will give you the desires of your heart—meaning you'll be given greater passion for God and for the work that's been planted in your heart.

It's a win-win-win situation for God and you and the people to whom you're being sent to serve with a joyful heart.

Mission Impossible

Do you recall the popular television and movie series *Mission Impossible*? The plot always revolved around secret agents on stealth assignments. "Your mission, should you decide to accept it...."

Well, your mission (which is your most unique life purpose), should you decide to accept it, is to deliver a deliberate message to a designated group of people. Although this isn't a stealth mission and this book won't self-destruct in five seconds, you're being called to perform a spectacular feat. That noble mission is to deliver a message from God in an effort to save somebody in the world from danger, sin, or a life of purposelessness—a life without the best that Jesus has to offer them.

That is your mission—to deliver the life message God wrote for you—to a certain group of people, just like God chose Isaiah to carry a specific message to a particular group of people, the Jews, to exhort them to turn from sin and repent from their idol worship.

Isaiah's response to God in Isaiah 6:8 was simple: *"Here I am. Send me."* Will Isaiah's response be your response when you're asked to carry a precise message to a distinct people group?

So, this Lifetime Dream Statement that you're expected to work on now—is it difficult to write? No, it's not hard at all, because you'll simply answer a few questions in these exercises, with the help of the Holy Spirit, to end up with a logical declaration! Not bad, huh? Think of it as a plug-and-play exercise, a fill-in-the-blank activity with lots of examples from which to choose! Your Lifetime Dream Statement will unfold before your eyes in these five steps:

- **Exercise #1:** What Group Is God Calling Me to Serve?

- **Exercise #2:** What's My Life Message or Power Slogan?

- **Exercise #3:** How Will I Get My Life Message Out?

- **Exercise #4:** What God-Inspired Passions Support My Mission?

- **Exercise #5: Plug in your answers from #1-4 to write your Statement!**

WHAT GROUP IS GOD CALLING ME TO SERVE?

Has God put a burden on your heart for a particular group of people? Have you ever wondered: "Could God possibly be calling me to serve that group?" Worded differently, in marketing terms: "Who's your target audience for ministry?"

Exercise #1: My Group of People

Instructions: Check or write one or two specific groups you feel God may be calling you to serve. (□ **P**arent □ **T**eenager)

Groups of People

P	T		P	T	
□	□	Abused Children	□	□	Actors
□	□	Addicts	□	□	Artists
□	□	Atheists	□	□	Athletes
□	□	Cancer Patients	□	□	Children With Special Needs
□	□	College Students	□	□	Depressed Youth
□	□	Disabled Veterans	□	□	Drug-Addicted Babies
□	□	Educators	□	□	Elderly
□	□	Engaged Couples	□	□	Executives
□	□	Families	□	□	Homeless
□	□	Hopeless	□	□	Illiterate
□	□	Immigrants	□	□	Law Enforcement
□	□	Military Families	□	□	Missionaries
□	□	Musicians	□	□	New Christians
□	□	Orphans	□	□	Parents
□	□	Pastors/Church Staff	□	□	Politicians
□	□	Poor/Hungry	□	□	Pregnant Girls
□	□	Prisoners	□	□	Rape Victims
□	□	Runaways	□	□	Shut-Ins
□	□	Single Parents	□	□	Teenagers
□	□	Unemployed	□	□	Youth Leaders
□	□	Other:			

Reflection Question about your call to serve a group:

- Which primary group do you feel God is calling you to serve? Why do you think that?

WHAT'S MY LIFE MESSAGE OR POWER SLOGAN?

Your life message is what you feel God is prompting you to say to the primary group of people you just noted in Exercise #1. Reflect on what you often hear yourself saying to others to encourage them. (For example, do you typically say something along these lines: *Don't worry* or *Imagine the new you* or *Jesus can work it out* or *Pray?*) Those types of often used remarks can point to the theme or heart of what God is asking you to tell the world. Think of your life message like a company tagline—like Nike's power slogan, *Just Do It*®. Your own God-inspired slogan will not only minister to others, but it'll also keep you focused and invite interested onlookers to come aboard to help you.

Examples of Taglines Companies Have Used:

The happiest place on earth® *(Disneyland)*   *We love to see you smile*® *(McDonald's)*
Leave the driving to us® *(Greyhound Bus)*   *We deliver for you*® *(U.S. Postal Service)*
Reach out and touch someone® *(AT&T)*   *You will never roam alone*® *(Travelocity)*

Examples of Christian Life Messages:

Hungry no more	*Come home to Jesus*	*Marriage matters*
Keeping it pure	*Full of grace*	*A new kind of healthy*
Take courage	*Everybody's somebody*	*It's time to talk*
Expect miracles	*Families coming together*	*Once and for all*
Your safe place to thrive	*The journey matters more*	*Sing your song*
When life hurts	*Peace—the real thing*	*He-brews a cup of faith 4U*
Reaching the unreached	*Be God-confident*	*Connect and live*
Never, ever give up	*Give more than you expect to receive*	

Exercise #2: My Life Message

Instructions for Writing Your Life Message: Write your creative life message below, using as few words as possible. Be bold and confident. *Don't try to guess your teenager's answer!* (**P**arent-**T**eenager)

My Life Message:
What I'd Like to Say to Those I'm Called to Serve

P _____

_____

T _____

_____

Reflection Question about your life message:

* What do you feel God is prompting you to say? Why do you think that?

HOW WILL I GET MY LIFE MESSAGE OUT?

What vision or impression do you have of how God might want you to deliver your God-inspired life message to your target audience—to your listeners? Ask yourself: "What's the ideal method for distributing or transporting my 'goods' (my message) to the marketplace I've been assigned?"

Exercise #3: My Delivery Methods

Instructions: Check or write all the delivery methods you feel may help you distribute your life message. (□ **Parent** □ **Teenager**)

Delivery Method Options
With examples of how each could work to get your message out!

I feel led/drawn/nudged/prompted to use...

P   T

☐   ☐   **My voice** (Moses and Aaron used their voices to challenge Pharaoh to release God's people from captivity in Egypt.) Give speeches; host a radio program; teach teachers; sing songs in a stadium; pray intercessory prayers with others worldwide; mentor or disciple

☐   ☐   **My written words** (The Gospel authors used the written word to spread the good news.) Write a book, article, letter, poem, song, brochure, strategic plan, marketing plan, website content, training manual, movie script, or legislative bill; be an editor

☐   ☐   **My money and possessions** (The woman from Shunem provided long-term housing and meals for the prophet Elisha.) Fund building projects for ministries; financially back the adoption of orphans; hire lobbyists to change laws; invite missionaries to a vacation spot for rest and renewal; support church plants and start-up ministries; "reverse tithe," which means giving away 90 percent of your income and living on 10 percent

☐   ☐   **My image/persona/charisma/looks** (Esther used her beauty, powers of persuasion, and prayerfulness to save her people from destruction.) Create a dynamic platform for others; conduct television interviews; perform in stage productions or movies; enlist celebrity help; be a spokesperson or a face for a cause; be an image adviser for Christian speakers; start a fashion model ministry

☐   ☐   **My ears** (Jesus listened and responded to the cries of those needing miracles.) Counsel clients; write music or play an instrument; shepherd small groups; listen to the lonely; use sound to create peaceful, inspiring environments for meditation; promote a class on turning a deaf ear to gossip

☐   ☐   **My hands/feet** (Noah obeyed God and built an ark.) Repair and build houses; shelter the abused; sew; clothe people; care for the ill and dying; perform open-heart surgery; sculpt; design mosaic windows; race mountain bikes to promote good health; open a horse stable as a community outreach; dig water wells in remote villages with no clean water supply

☐   ☐   **My eyes** (Mary Magdalene was the first to see Jesus after the Resurrection and proclaim, "I have seen the Lord!" to others.) Create "curb appeal" for churches to attract guests; replicate nature's beauty in art; see solutions for logistical problems at events; start a bird-watching ministry for non-Christians; volunteer for the blind; offer free optometry services to the uninsured poor

☐   ☐   **My mind** (King Solomon was the wisest man on earth and was chosen by God to oversee the building of the ancient Jerusalem Temple.) Lead; project manage; inspire/motivate; create theories; make discoveries; invent things; do vision-casting; prosecute; solve problems; develop a systematic approach for improvement

☐ ☐ **My sense of taste/smell and hospitality** (Martha and Mary, who between the two of them served others and honored Jesus.) Cater events; provide disaster relief meals; feed the homeless or refugees; create a perfume to raise funds

☐ ☐ **Other:**

Reflection Question about your delivery methods:

- Which one or two best delivery methods do you feel God is prompting you to use for the distribution of your message? Why do you think that?

WHAT GOD-INSPIRED PASSIONS SUPPORT MY LIFE MISSION?

Your God-inspired passions are the sizzle and zest that have been wired into you and make you want to jump out of bed in the morning to focus on them. They reflect your most creative self and deepest longings, causing you to lose track of time. God has embedded several healthy passions in you, not only to guarantee you some renewed gusto when your day-to-day life gets difficult, but also to enliven your lifetime dream itself.

Exercise #4: My God-Inspired Passions

Instructions: Check all the God-inspired or healthy passions that apply to you. (☐ **P**arent ☐ **T**eenager.) Make sure to write any other passions you've noticed during this series, such as a...

- Spiritual Gift—like leadership, evangelism, teaching, or writing

- Finest Value—like social justice, health, teamwork, or truth

- Strength—like acting, computer programming, gardening, or photography

God-Inspired Passions (The Pizzazz of Life!)

P	T		P	T	
☐	☐	Antiques	☐	☐	Baseball Cards
☐	☐	Cake Decorating	☐	☐	Child Safety Laws
☐	☐	Craft Projects	☐	☐	Crossword Puzzles
☐	☐	Curing a Disease	☐	☐	Current Events/Politics
☐	☐	Dancing	☐	☐	Dignity of Life
☐	☐	Discipleship	☐	☐	Education/Learning
☐	☐	Environment/Nature	☐	☐	Farming/Livestock
☐	☐	Fashion/Styling	☐	☐	Football/Boxing
☐	☐	Gourmet Cooking	☐	☐	Guitar/Drums/Flute
☐	☐	History/Archaeology	☐	☐	Human Rights
☐	☐	Human Suffering	☐	☐	Immigrants/Homeless
☐	☐	Interior/Graphic Design	☐	☐	International Travel
☐	☐	Literature/Cultures	☐	☐	Makeovers
☐	☐	Marathons/Bicycling	☐	☐	Martial Arts/Pilates
☐	☐	Modeling	☐	☐	Musicals/Theatre
☐	☐	Mystery Novels	☐	☐	Overseas Mission Trips
☐	☐	Physical Fitness	☐	☐	Poverty Issues
☐	☐	Pro-Life Advocacy	☐	☐	Public Relations
☐	☐	Rain Forests/Wildlife	☐	☐	Recovery Program
☐	☐	Remodeling Houses	☐	☐	Recycling
☐	☐	Science Experiments	☐	☐	Technology Apps
☐	☐	Textiles/Embroidery/Quilting	☐	☐	Trains/Cars/Boats/Planes
☐	☐	TV/Movie Decency Ratings	☐	☐	Video Games
☐	☐	Water/Outdoor Sports	☐	☐	Other:

Reflection Question about your passions:

- What possibility do you see about how one or two of your passions could be used by God?

WRITE MY LIFETIME DREAM STATEMENT

(Also known as *My Life Mission Statement* or *Unique Life Purpose Statement*)

To complete your written statement, you'll be instructed to plug in your answers from Exercises 1-2-3-4, but first, check out these samples to get a look at some finished products!

SAMPLE #1: MY LIFETIME DREAM STATEMENT

My God-Inspired, Unique Life Purpose Is to...

MY TARGET AUDIENCE:

• Tell *single mothers...*

MY LIFE MESSAGE:

• *"Don't give up hope!"*

MY DELIVERY METHOD:

• I'll *use my voice* on the radio, and I'll also *use my written words* in a book to get God's message of hope out worldwide.

MY PASSION/PIZZAZZ!

• At times, I'll incorporate these passions into my ministry design for this reason: *Fashion* and *image makeovers*—to create a fun ambience, as the women learn about their hope in Christ.

SAMPLE #2: MY LIFETIME DREAM STATEMENT

My God-Inspired, Unique Life Purpose Is to...

MY TARGET AUDIENCE:

• Tell *college-age men...*

MY LIFE MESSAGE:

• *"Honesty matters."*

MY DELIVERY METHOD:

• I'll *use my eyes* to create the graphic design of a heavily publicized website that disciples young men in our tri-county area to understand the importance of integrity in all they say and do. And I'll use my money to create a statewide network of church and campus pastors involved in our mission. This includes funding the costs of monthly meetings and related travel, as well as their recommended projects.

MY PASSION/PIZZAZZ!

• At times, I'll incorporate these passions into my ministry design for this reason: *Rock-climbing* and *scuba diving*—to help emphasize that becoming more authentic is a great adventure.

Mother Teresa's Lifetime Dream Statement
(We can easily build this statement from what we know about her life and calling!)

My God-Inspired, Unique Life Purpose Is to...

MY TARGET AUDIENCE:

• Tell the *poorest of the poor*, including refugees, ex-prostitutes, the mentally ill, abandoned children, lepers, AIDS victims, and the aged, sick, and dying...

MY LIFE MESSAGE:

• *"Jesus loves you."*

MY DELIVERY METHOD:

• I'll *use my hands* to feed, clothe, and shelter the hurting, and I'll also *use my mind* to cast vision, lead, and inspire others to help me worldwide.

MY PASSION/PIZZAZZ!

• At all times, I'll incorporate these passions into my ministry design for this reason: The *dignity of life* and the *relief of human suffering in the name of Jesus*—to love others and help draw them to Christ.

Exercise #5: My Lifetime Dream Statement

Instructions: Fill in your name at the top. Then write your Lifetime Dream Statement by plugging in your answers from the four exercises you just finished. Notice the extra Lifetime Dream Statement for your teenager; don't try to guess the answers!

1. **MY TARGET AUDIENCE:** Plug in the group God has called you to serve.

2. **MY LIFE MESSAGE:** Plug in your God-breathed life message.

3. **MY DELIVERY METHOD:** Plug in your God-designed delivery method.

4. **MY PASSION:** Plug in your God-inspired, personal pizzazz for this mission.

MY LIFETIME DREAM STATEMENT (PARENT)

Name: _____

Considering everything God has revealed to me about my…

- Spiritual Gifts, Best Qualities, and Finest Values

- Motives, Relationships, and Use of Time

- Strengths, Weaknesses, Opportunities, and Threats

- Courage, Perseverance, and Expectation of Miracles

My God-Inspired, Unique Life Purpose Is to…

MY TARGET AUDIENCE:

• Tell…

MY LIFE MESSAGE:

•

MY DELIVERY METHOD:

• I'll use

MY PASSION/PIZZAZZ!

• At times, I'll incorporate these passions into my ministry design for this reason:

Considering this unique call on my life from God, I commit this month to taking this baby step toward my lifetime dream:

If I inherited $6 billion, this is what I'd do with the money to complete my lifetime dream—after I paid taxes, tithed to my church, helped my family and friends a lot, bought some stuff, and/or took a few great vacations!

My Signature _____
Date _____

Conversation Partner Witness _____
Date _____

MY LIFETIME DREAM STATEMENT (TEENAGER)

Name: _____

Considering everything God has revealed to me about my…

- Spiritual Gifts, Best Qualities, and Finest Values

- Motives, Relationships, and Use of Time

- Strengths, Weaknesses, Opportunities, and Threats

- Courage, Perseverance, and Expectation of Miracles

My God-Inspired, Unique Life Purpose Is to…

MY TARGET AUDIENCE:

• Tell…

MY LIFE MESSAGE:

•

MY DELIVERY METHOD:

• I'll use

MY PASSION/PIZZAZZ!

• At times, I'll incorporate these passions into my ministry design for this reason:

Considering this unique call on my life from God, I commit this month to taking this baby step toward my lifetime dream:

If I inherited $6 billion, this is what I'd do with the money to complete my lifetime dream—after I paid taxes, tithed to my church, helped my family and friends a lot, bought some stuff, and/or took a few great vacations!

My Signature _____
Date _____

Conversation Partner Witness _____
Date _____

135

Sign each other's Lifetime Dream Statement.

Reflection Questions about your Lifetime Dream Statement:

1. What has God revealed to you about your lifetime dream?

2. How do you feel about your unique life purpose and the baby step you wrote?

3. What would you do with a $6 billion inheritance?

Will You?

Assuming that you've been brave enough to ask God to reveal your bold life calling and to write out your Lifetime Dream Statement, congratulations—you can now move confidently toward your life mission! Will you, for the rest of your life, prayerfully, humbly, and obediently be receptive to God's step-by-step instructions for completing the work you've been assigned? Starting now, how will your insight about how you were wired with a lifetime dream (eons ago!) affect your day-to-day living and the fulfillment of your unique life mission?

To wrap up your parent-teenager conversation with intentionality:

- **Encourage your teenager to summarize his insights, by asking a question like this:** *Starting now, how will your insight about how you were wired with a lifetime dream (eons ago!) affect your day-to-day living and the fulfillment of your unique life mission?*

- **Challenge your teenager and yourself to memorize the verse at the beginning of this chapter.**

- **Affirm with a positive statement about who your teenager is in Christ.**

- **Close by personalizing a brief prayer, like this:**

  God, how can we ever thank you for loving us enough to give us a lifetime dream and perfectly wiring us to complete it? Please accept our humble gratitude. Although we'll need your constant guidance, resources, and support system to follow our life calling, we're blessed beyond measure to be taking our first step toward it, by being able to see it in writing. Thank you for who you are and for the unique life purpose you've given us. In Jesus' name we pray. Amen.

  Also, keep praying that the Holy Spirit will reveal your life verse. Tell your teenager (and vice versa), if you think you've found it!

CHAPTER 10
SURRENDERING ALL TO JESUS

So here's what I want you to do, God helping you: Take your everyday, ordinary life—your sleeping, eating, going-to-work, and walking-around life—and place it before God as an offering (Romans 12:1 The Message).

God Wants It All

Over the past 20 to 30 years, I've surrendered to God more than you may be prepared to hear, so brace yourself—some of it's as ugly as sin. Here are a few things I've felt led to leave at the foot of Jesus' cross:

- Smoking—when I understood the damage it was doing to my body, God's Temple

- Drinking—when I realized God was calling me into a ministry leadership position

- Cursing—when it was evident that my swearing would eventually lead to me taking Jesus' name in vain, and I knew that would break my heart

- Rage—when I grieved over the poor role modeling I was doing for my children

- My Home—when I knew for sure that there was more to life than possessions

- Income—when I learned that I was only a steward of all God has given me

- Children and Grandchildren—when it became crystal clear to me that God can take better care of them than I can (well, I'm still working on surrendering my two grandsons!)

- Reputation—when I began to believe that my sufficiency rests only in Christ

- Lifetime Dream—when my dream was dead, and it was obvious to me that if God didn't choose to resurrect it, I didn't have any desire for it

As you may have gathered, these were all things I was prompted to surrender, not forced to surrender. Notice the verbs and phrases, such as *understood, realized, it was evident, grieved, knew for sure, learned, became crystal clear, began to believe,* and *it was obvious.* The things I finally surrendered were things the Holy Spirit guided me to investigate logically before I made a cognitive decision. No coercion was involved, although I made sure there was lots of unnecessary emotion and drama.

You can see that I was one angry woman for a long period of my life—even as a supposedly "good Christian." I had stuff the Lord needed to purge out of me. We all have issues, and God is waiting for us (me, you, your teenager) to surrender our latest or most long-standing issues and blessings, too. As you work through this last chapter, consider surrendering all, including your life's dream, to the King and Ruler of the universe. You really have nothing to lose, because God is faithful in all things and has an incredible plan for you and your teenager that will make all your current dreams look like child's play! You simply can't out-dream God.

Best Practice #6

We've been focusing on six methods to help you understand and complete the remarkable assignment God has entrusted to you. The capstone or high point is this best practice, **Surrendering All to Jesus**, because no life mission in the world matters unless it's surrendered completely to God.

Tip about how to cooperate with God's plan: If I surrender my life to Jesus, acknowledging my role as a humble steward of all I've been asked to manage on earth, God will be glorified and I'll be blessed. (And the same is true for your teenager!)

Special Activity for Chapter 10: Personal Surrender Exercise

This chapter is divided into two parts: the explanatory/teaching segment and the Personal Surrender Exercise. There's no parent-teenager conversation related to this material; instead, your conversation partner for the exercise is Jesus! The purpose of this time is to surrender back to Jesus such things as your fears, motives, strengths, weaknesses, relationships, spiritual gifts, possessions, and lifetime dream.

So, here's a reminder of a Chapter 2 suggestion: You might want to consider arranging a special 50- to 60-minute solitude retreat for yourself and your teenager to do the Surrender Exercise at the same time but quite independent of one another. This private, uninterrupted time of quiet reflection can be in your own home or at one of your favorite places such as a local park, lake, cabin, or beach. Prepare your heart now for this compelling exercise that can be life-changing for one or both of you. (See also in that chapter: *Note from my heart, as a mother and a professional Life Purpose Coach®.*)

How to Help Your Teenager Have the Best Possible Surrender Exercise

Follow these guidelines:

1. Let your teenager know the gist of this chapter and that there's no parent-teenager conversation. You can discuss whether one or both of you would like to do the Personal Surrender Exercise at home or turn the exercise into a special outing. It's really about a surrendered heart, not about the perfect location—so be careful not to go overboard, piling on the pressure to have a perfect surrender experience.

2. As you hand off this book to your teenager, encourage her to read the opening remarks of the chapter and the topical explanation that's prior to the exercise. Or you can offer to give a brief overview of this chapter's topic and to answer any related questions.

3. This book has two copies of the Surrender Exercise and also two copies of the Certificate of Surrender. But if you're planning on doing the exercise at the same time, you or your teenager will need to download those two documents from our website and print them. (The certificate is available in color!)

4. Don't try to guess any of your teenager's answers. Let her know that the Surrender Exercise is private, between Jesus and her only. Mention, too, that you won't be asking any questions out of curiosity—although she's free to share anything she'd like.

5. If your teenager has her own separate copy of the Surrender Exercise and Certificate of Surrender, rather than the book, she may use any color ink.

6. When it's time for one or both of you to do the Surrender Exercise, personalize a brief prayer, like this:

Jesus, thank you that you'll be sitting with each of us privately to discuss what you'd like us to surrender. We pray for peace that far surpasses understanding as we make some hard decisions about the people we're becoming. We do want to move forward to fulfill your outstanding plan for our lives, based on how you've wired us. Holy Spirit, we're very aware that the work that'll be done here isn't solely up to us—and that we need to rely on your power. Amen.

7. For your closing prayer, you'll be instructed to use the Certificate of Surrender, as a final prayer exercise.

Also, keep praying that the Holy Spirit will reveal your life verse. Tell your teenager (and vice versa), if you think you've found it!

You might be wondering, "What's all this talk about surrender?" In general, surrender signifies your willingness to give something to Jesus—to entrust it to the care of our kind and all knowing Lord. It means that you're ready to wave the white flag of surrender to the Ruler of the universe, releasing your control to God. It means that you believe that God can and will do a better job than you in a given area, like with your children, finances, disappointments, or impatience. Surrendering your life and dreams to Jesus becomes the key to living out the plan that's been designed uniquely for you.

Let's look at some details that will help you make a fully informed, private, unpressured decision about what you might choose to surrender at this time.

Salvation vs. Surrender

So, what's the difference between **salvation** and **surrender**?

Salvation is inviting Jesus Christ to be the **Savior** of your life. Don't be shy about letting a church leader or Christian friend know if you have some questions. Answering your questions is why they're there—why they were born.

Surrender is voluntarily granting Jesus **Lordship** or control over all areas of your life. It becomes a daily response to the pursuit of the Holy Spirit, as you learn truths that allow you to give up control, power, and possessions of your life. Wikipedia defines the word "surrender" as *the relinquishment of one's own will.* It means that you are surrendering to the authority of another because he or she demands it.

Although God won't go against your free will and demand that you surrender while you're on earth, everyone will surrender on Judgment Day. The Bible tells us that even *The mighty deep cried out, lifting its hands to the Lord (Habakkuk 3:10).*

Do you remember another great Scripture that talks about this same idea? *Therefore, God elevated him to the place of highest honor and gave him the name above all other names, that at the name of Jesus every knee should bow, in heaven and on earth and under the earth, and every tongue confess that Jesus Christ is Lord, to the glory of God the Father (Philippians 2:9-11).*

So, the question isn't, "Will you surrender?"—but rather, "When will you surrender?" That truth makes right now a good moment, hour, day, week, month, and year to surrender.

What is the purpose of surrender?

We surrender as a humble, grateful steward of God's unique plan for our life, so we can produce fruit for the kingdom, which brings glory to God.

*"You didn't choose me. I chose you. I appointed you to go and **produce lasting fruit**, so that the Father will give you whatever you ask for, using my name" (John 15:16, emphasis added).*

*Then the way you live will always honor and please the Lord, and your lives **will produce every kind of good fruit** (Colossians 1:10, emphasis added).*

How does the Holy Spirit help me surrender?

The Holy Spirit, your ultimate guidance counselor, has many ways to get your attention when it comes to surrender. For example, you may...

- receive a higher calling like parenting or experience a noble reason you can't ignore, such a call to lay ministry work, both of which make surrender crucial.

- experience consequences (from something like alcohol abuse, adultery, credit card debt, or pride) that cause you to think about what you're doing with your life, trying to run it on your own terms.

- feel a deepening of your love for Jesus that inspires you to surrender your talents, exhaustion, retirement plans, church pew, greed, or hobby.

Regardless of the Holy Spirit's method, you won't have to muscle up to do it; instead, the Lord of Heaven's Armies will be there to help you.

How much will it cost me to surrender?

It could cost you everything. God may choose to take what you offer, so don't begin to surrender until you count the cost of what you may lose.

Here's what Jesus said in Luke 14:28 about the cost of being a disciple: *"But don't begin until you count the cost. For who would begin construction of a building without first calculating the cost to see if there is enough money to finish it?"*

Who else has surrendered?

Among many others listed in the Bible and throughout the ages, three of the most extreme cases of surrender have been a humble servant girl, three kings, and Jesus.

- **Mary**, who surrendered unconditionally to God's will, said this: *"I'm the Lord's maid, ready to serve. Let it be with me just as you say"* (Luke 1:38 The Message).

- **Three Kings**, to whom it was revealed that Jesus was not going to be crowned as Israel's earthly king, as they had first thought, but would be Christ the King of heaven and earth: *When they saw the star, they were filled with joy! They entered the house and saw the child with his mother, Mary, and they bowed down and worshiped him. Then they opened their treasure chests and gave him gifts of gold, frankincense, and myrrh (Matthew 2:10-11).*

- **Jesus**, who surrendered to God, when crying out in the Garden of Gethsemane: *"My Father! If it is possible, let this cup of suffering be taken away from me. Yet I want your will to be done, not mine"* (Matthew 26:39).

How do I surrender?

To surrender anything, such as your shame, grief, personal timetable, or health, it's important to take five action steps to turn your will over to the will of God:

Step 1: REVELATION: Seek the truth. Be still and quiet your soul. Ask the Holy Spirit to reveal the truth of each situation to you.

Step 2: INVESTIGATION: Do your footwork and homework. Do your research, make a phone call, read a book, speak with a counselor, listen to a sermon, or do whatever will help you make a logical decision. Key point: We investigate using the brain God gave us, because surrender is intended to be a thought process more than a heart matter. God isn't looking for an emotional response but for a logical and well thought-out commitment, so you can never say you were emotionally coerced. Surrender is your informed decision—although a Kleenex® or two has been known to be involved for those types who cry at weddings!

Step 3: CALCULATION: Count the cost. Be aware of what might change in your life if God does decide to take what you've surrendered. This is usually the most difficult step, so be kind to yourself. Think this step through carefully.

Step 4: DECLARATION: Humbly state that you're giving up control of your own will to focus on Jesus. Write your decision, tell someone, or have a declaration ceremony. For example, have you ever thrown stones into the ocean to release some feelings? That action also works great to release surrender items. At retreats, women often lay things at the foot of a cross—whereas, men like to burn the Post-it® Notes that list their surrender items. I've heard that mud baths at a spa work really well, too, to symbolize a clean, new life! Regardless of how you choose to write, speak, or experience your surrender declaration, just remember that the point is to let go of your heavy burden as top dog of your universe, so you can fix your attention on Jesus.

Step 5: TRANSFORMATION: Trust Almighty God to be God, as you become changed from the inside out. Remember all God's previous provisions and miracles in your life, and keep your eyes set on holiness. Begin anew to grow in your faith.

CHAPTER 6 EXERCISE: SURRENDER

Instructions: Enjoy your Personal Surrender Exercise: Imagine that you're sitting alone with Jesus! Be still. Take your time to read the Letter From Jesus and respond however the Holy Spirit prompts you. Don't put a lot of expectations on yourself for the outcome. Just be open, relaxed, and confident that Jesus is thrilled to be chatting with you in this private setting. Focus on the grace, joy, peace, and wisdom that are yours for the asking!

Logistics of how to respond to Jesus: It may help you to circle key phrases that stand out to you as you read the letter. Or using the blank spaces, feel free to draw a picture, write a song or poem, journal your thoughts, or compose a text message to Jesus as you pray for revelation about what to surrender and for insight about how that surrender will affect your awesome life mission. You may want to give each "blank space" entry a title. *Notice the extra Surrender Exercise document for your teenager. Don't try to guess your teenager's answers!*

CHAPTER 6 EXERCISE: CERTIFICATE

Instructions: Fill in the "Certificate of Surrender." Use this as your closing prayer. Notice the extra Certificate of Surrender for your teenager. Don't try to guess your teenager's answers! If you'd like extra color copies of this keepsake document, visit simplyyouthministry.com.

PERSONAL SURRENDER EXERCISE (PARENT)

"Be still, and know that I am God! I will be honored by every nation. I will be honored throughout the world" (Psalm 46:10).

Don't Pray: *God, please do this for me.*

Don't Pray: *God, I'm going to do this for you.*

Don't Pray: *God, I really want you to use me, but I need details.*

PRAY: *God, use me up for your glory—all of me. In your wisdom, reveal any details on an as-needed basis: where, when, what, how, with whom, and for whom! I can live without these answers: why and for how long. I surrender to you—all of me—now. Use me up.*

God has called you to a super-sized assignment! You may feel inadequate. Will you surrender that feeling to Jesus and become completely dependent upon God to make you able? What about other areas in which you're feeling a nudge to surrender? Prayerfully read and respond to these varied scenarios about surrendering your life to the Lord of all.

A Letter From Jesus:

Yes, someone else may be a better speaker or writer or encourager than you are. But don't you see that I called you to this particular task? *Surrender to me your spirit of defeat, self-doubt, and jealousy of others. Surrender your fear of failure, success, and rejection—all fears that paralyze you.* Allow me to replace those feelings with my vision of who you are, with the courage only I can give. You're my *poiēma*, my workmanship. You're my *magnum opus*, my magnificent masterpiece.

So, you don't feel you're good enough in your ministry interactions. Why are you focused on yourself during service opportunities? *Surrender to me your feelings of unworthiness, perfectionism, wrong motives, personality quirks, and concern of how you appear to others when you minister.* Allow yourself simply to show up where I'm at work, becoming virtually invisible, as I receive the attention, honor, and glory.

Surrender to me your idea of success and let me show you what prosperity in me looks like. Allow me to prosper you far beyond what you could ever dream or imagine. I'm not promising you earthly riches, but what I'll give you in return for your surrender is an abundant life of fulfillment and joy.

[My thoughts, frustrations, and prayers...]

Thank you for your willingness to obey me, by taking on a ministry leadership role. Now, I simply ask you to wait. The timing for this to fully unfold isn't yet right. I cherish your excitement and anticipation to get started, but *I want you to surrender to me your timetable and your gift of leadership.* Allow me to work at my perfect pace. While you wait, please enjoy the fun times of watching me build your personal relationships, platform, network, resources, and skills.

I see you. Obviously, I've seen you and have known you since before the world began. Nothing in your past, present, or future is hidden from me. *Surrender to me your secrets, shame and guilt, people-pleasing, need to be right, and control issues.* Only in my mirror do you appear fully mature and equipped for the mission I've assigned to your life.

Although you're involved in many good things, *I want you to surrender to me your life roles, household responsibilities, and job—along with your high personal expectations.* Allow me to weed out anything—even good things—that hinder you from completely following my best plans for you. *Yes, I also want you to surrender your devotional time, small group, and accountability partner.*

My precious one, I understand the deepest pain you feel. When you're hurting, I'm closer to you than the air you breathe. *Surrender to me the "Why" questions you have regarding your sorrows.* Rest on my promise that I'm a loving God and that I'm working all things together for your good. Give me your impatience and your depression, while you wait prayerfully for a solution.

Of course, I realize that you have food, shelter, and clothing needs, as well as safety and security concerns. *Surrender those things to me and allow me to be the One who grants you every provision you need.* I'm honored when you say, "Lord, if you don't meet this need in the way I've narrowly prescribed, I'll still choose to glorify you with my life." Do your part, as I've asked you to do, and then expect that I'll provide for your every need—miraculously!

I see the weight on your shoulders. I know you're exhausted. Come to me, just as you are—weary and heavy-laden, and I promise to give you rest. I'll renew your spirit. *Surrender to me your fatigue, your exhaustion.* My yoke is easy and my burden is light. I'm the reason you'll be able to persevere.

Surrender to me each of your family members and friends by name. Yes, give me the young and the elderly; give me those with whom you're struggling relationally; give me those who are in crisis emotionally, spiritually, physically, or financially; give me your social networking relationships. You know that I can certainly take better care of them than you can.

And surrender to me, too, your tendency to be a lone ranger in certain areas of your life. I completely understand that this presents a huge step of faith for you, so trust that I won't disappoint you. I'm the One who will send you a team to surround you and carry you through.

[My thoughts, frustrations, and prayers...]

I, too, feel your pain regarding your past. I love you infinitely more than you could possibly imagine. *Surrender to me all your pain—the abuse, neglect, poor choices, grief, loss, lies, crises, and disappointments.* I know, I know, I know—how you've ached over your troubles! Give me your hurts and hang-ups. Listen for my guidance in the days ahead.

I see your loneliness. I hear you as you cry out to me from that dark, lonely room in the middle of another sleepless night. *Surrender to me your tears.* Allow me to fill those empty places in your life with my hope, light, and companionship. Your sadness requires that you trust me all the more.

Surrender to me your now. The circumstances you find yourself in now may not make sense to you. Give me that confusion, that lack of clarity. Allow me to strengthen you to do each of your *todays* with pure joy. Lean on me. Let my arms encircle you. I love you. Release, even all of this, to me.

I see that illness in your body. I see the brokenness you face. *Surrender to me your health.* I'm the Great Physician. I can instantaneously heal you or show doctors how to cure you, but I want you to trust me to do what's best for you at this time.

Surrender to me your thoughts. I deeply desire to transform your mind with my thoughts. Don't allow the impure, negative, or anxious thoughts of your human nature to destroy you. Focus your eyes on me and stop rehearsing your anger. I'm here for you. I want to give you victory over your regrets—over all that haunts you in the privacy of your mind.

I see that stronghold—the one specific thing that keeps you defeated. Give it to me. *Surrender to me that which is weighing you down, and allow me to release you from it.* I want your sins—your overspending and overreacting, as well as your gossip, unforgiving spirit, bragging, and sex outside the boundaries of marriage. Nothing is impossible for me! Focus on what it'll feel like to be set free. I paid for your sins by my death on the cross, so you could be buried with me and raised to live a brand-new life. Release your sins now, so you can begin to soar on eagles' wings.

[My thoughts, frustrations, and prayers...]

Surrender to me your next steps in the completion of your goals. Only I can see the view of your life from beginning to end. I'm the Alpha and the Omega. I have mighty plans for you that require your cooperation and obedience to my will. Allow my Spirit to lead you on a daily, hourly, and minute-by-minute basis.

I'm a jealous God. *Surrender to me anything that takes precedence in your life:* your love of money, your need to be appreciated and recognized, and your need to fit in. I want your strengths, spiritual gifts, values, and opportunities—anything that you place above me. Give it all to me. I want all the methods you rely on to numb the pain in your life— alcohol, drugs, nicotine, food, shopping, drama, dangerous stunts, and hoarding. None of it will ever satisfy you like I can. I'll have no other gods above me.

I value your passion for my calling on your life. But my dear one, this is my work. *Surrender to me your lifetime dream and your need to feel significant, to make a difference in this world, to matter, to be heard.* I'll be faithful to complete my work, and equally important, I'll be faithful to complete my work in you in my miraculous way and with my timing.

Do you now understand that what I want is you? Not only the parts you choose to give me; not only the parts you can't seem to *make better*; not only the parts you dislike—but all of you. More than anything, I want you in a loving and intimate relationship with me. I want to grow you into spiritual maturity, into a likeness of me. I want to see your faith increase as you experience me in every aspect of your life. *I'm asking you to surrender to me—all of you—now.*

Will you surrender to me all of you, including your lifetime dream?

Will You?

Your Memory Verse, Romans 12:1, reminds you to place your life before God as a living sacrifice. It reads this way from The Message paraphrase:

So here's what I want you to do, God helping you: Take your everyday, ordinary life—your sleeping, eating, going-to-work, and walking-around life—and place it before God as an offering.

What if Jesus actually has whispered a few good ideas to you in this chapter about what to surrender? What if you really were able to acknowledge your role as a humble steward of all God has asked you to manage on earth? Will you, in preparation for your life mission, move forward in at least one area of surrender? In what way will your prayerful insight about surrender specifically impact your day-to-day living and unique life mission—now?

CERTIFICATE OF SURRENDER (PARENT)

The earth is the Lord's, and everything in it. The world and all its people belong to him (Psalm 24:1 NLT).

Pray the following prayer if you're ready to surrender one or more things. Take this step at your own pace, without feeling rushed or pressured into it. This is between Jesus and you only.

I Surrender Now

Dear Jesus,

I've counted the cost of surrendering the things I've indicated as I read your letter. I know full well that you may, indeed, take one or more of these things from me, literally. I understand that if you do, it's my responsibility to trust and obey you on a daily, hourly, and minute-by-minute basis. I know that you're acutely aware of how important these things are to me. I love you unconditionally as my Almighty Lord.

In your holy name, I surrender to you these things. Amen.

Signature: _____ Date: _____

Continue praying this prayer if you're ready to surrender everything:

Jesus, I'm content with whatever you choose to give to me or take from me, whether you decide to bless me anymore or not. Everything I have belongs to you, so I leave it all in your hands. Give me the grace to never stop loving you, even if I...

- Lose everything, family and friends included

- Am dirt poor

- Become terminally ill

- Will never be considered a success

- Will never see my dreams come true

- Will never feel like I'm making a profound difference in the world

I freely empty myself of everything except you, so I can be filled by you. I surrender to you all of me, including my lifetime dream.

Your Initials: _____

PERSONAL SURRENDER EXERCISE (TEENAGER)

"Be still, and know that I am God! I will be honored by every nation. I will be honored throughout the world" (Psalm 46:10).

Don't Pray: *God, please do this for me.*

Don't Pray: *God, I'm going to do this for you.*

Don't Pray: *God, I really want you to use me, but I need details.*

PRAY: *God, use me up for your glory—all of me. In your wisdom, reveal any details on an as-needed basis: where, when, what, how, with whom, and for whom! I can live without these answers: why and for how long. I surrender to you—all of me—now. Use me up.*

God has called you to a super-sized assignment! You may feel inadequate. Will you surrender that feeling to Jesus and become completely dependent upon God to make you able? What about other areas in which you're feeling a nudge to surrender? Prayerfully read and respond to these varied scenarios about surrendering your life to the Lord of all.

A Letter From Jesus:

Yes, someone else may be a better speaker or writer or encourager than you are. But don't you see that I called you to this particular task? *Surrender to me your spirit of defeat, self-doubt, and jealousy of others. Surrender your fear of failure, success, and rejection—all fears that paralyze you.* Allow me to replace those feelings with my vision of who you are, with the courage only I can give. You're my *poiēma*, my workmanship. You're my *magnum opus*, my magnificent masterpiece.

So, you don't feel you're good enough in your ministry interactions. Why are you focused on yourself during service opportunities? *Surrender to me your feelings of unworthiness, perfectionism, wrong motives, personality quirks, and concern of how you appear to others when you minister.* Allow yourself simply to show up where I'm at work, becoming virtually invisible, as I receive the attention, honor, and glory.

Surrender to me your idea of success and let me show you what prosperity in me looks like. Allow me to prosper you far beyond what you could ever dream or imagine. I'm not promising you earthly riches, but what I'll give you in return for your surrender is an abundant life of fulfillment and joy.

[My thoughts, frustrations, and prayers...]

Thank you for your willingness to obey me, by taking on a ministry leadership role. Now, I simply ask you to wait. The timing for this to fully unfold isn't yet right. I cherish your excitement and anticipation to get started, but *I want you to surrender to me your timetable and your gift of leadership.* Allow me to work at my perfect pace. While you wait, please enjoy the fun times of watching me build your personal relationships, platform, network, resources, and skills.

I see you. Obviously, I've seen you and have known you since before the world began. Nothing in your past, present, or future is hidden from me. *Surrender to me your secrets, shame and guilt, people-pleasing, need to be right, and control issues.* Only in my mirror do you appear fully mature and equipped for the mission I've assigned to your life.

Although you're involved in many good things, *I want you to surrender to me your life roles, household responsibilities, and job—along with your high personal expectations.* Allow me to weed out anything—even good things—that hinder you from completely following my best plans for you. *Yes, I also want you to surrender your devotional time, small group, and accountability partner.*

My precious one, I understand the deepest pain you feel. When you're hurting, I'm closer to you than the air you breathe. *Surrender to me the "Why" questions you have regarding your sorrows.* Rest on my promise that I'm a loving God and that I'm working all things together for your good. Give me your impatience and your depression, while you wait prayerfully for a solution.

Of course, I realize that you have food, shelter, and clothing needs, as well as safety and security concerns. *Surrender those things to me and allow me to be the One who grants you every provision you need.* I'm honored when you say, "Lord, if you don't meet this need in the way I've narrowly prescribed, I'll still choose to glorify you with my life." Do your part, as I've asked you to do, and then expect that I'll provide for your every need—miraculously!

I see the weight on your shoulders. I know you're exhausted. Come to me, just as you are—weary and heavy-laden, and I promise to give you rest. I'll renew your spirit. *Surrender to me your fatigue, your exhaustion.* My yoke is easy and my burden is light. I'm the reason you'll be able to persevere.

Surrender to me each of your family members and friends by name. Yes, give me the young and the elderly; give me those with whom you're struggling relationally; give me those who are in crisis emotionally, spiritually, physically, or financially; give me your social networking relationships. You know that I can certainly take better care of them than you can.

And surrender to me, too, your tendency to be a lone ranger in certain areas of your life. I completely understand that this presents a huge step of faith for you, so trust that I won't disappoint you. I'm the One who will send you a team to surround you and carry you through.

[My thoughts, frustrations, and prayers...]

I, too, feel your pain regarding your past. I love you infinitely more than you could possibly imagine. *Surrender to me all your pain—the abuse, neglect, poor choices, grief, loss, lies, crises, and disappointments.* I know, I know, I know—how you've ached over your troubles! Give me your hurts and hang-ups. Listen for my guidance in the days ahead.

I see your loneliness. I hear you as you cry out to me from that dark, lonely room in the middle of another sleepless night. *Surrender to me your tears.* Allow me to fill those empty places in your life with my hope, light, and companionship. Your sadness requires that you trust me all the more.

Surrender to me your now. The circumstances you find yourself in now may not make sense to you. Give me that confusion, that lack of clarity. Allow me to strengthen you to do each of your *todays* with pure joy. Lean on me. Let my arms encircle you. I love you. Release, even all of this, to me.

I see that illness in your body. I see the brokenness you face. *Surrender to me your health.* I'm the Great Physician. I can instantaneously heal you or show doctors how to cure you, but I want you to trust me to do what's best for you at this time.

Surrender to me your thoughts. I deeply desire to transform your mind with my thoughts. Don't allow the impure, negative, or anxious thoughts of your human nature to destroy you. Focus your eyes on me and stop rehearsing your anger. I'm here for you. I want to give you victory over your regrets—over all that haunts you in the privacy of your mind.

I see that stronghold—the one specific thing that keeps you defeated. Give it to me. *Surrender to me that which is weighing you down, and allow me to release you from it.* I want your sins—your overspending and overreacting, as well as your gossip, unforgiving spirit, bragging, and sex outside the boundaries of marriage. Nothing is impossible for me! Focus on what it'll feel like to be set free. I paid for your sins by my death on the cross, so you could be buried with me and raised to live a brand-new life. Release your sins now, so you can begin to soar on eagles' wings.

[My thoughts, frustrations, and prayers...]

Surrender to me your next steps in the completion of your goals. Only I can see the view of your life from beginning to end. I'm the Alpha and the Omega. I have mighty plans for you that require your cooperation and obedience to my will. Allow my Spirit to lead you on a daily, hourly, and minute-by-minute basis.

I'm a jealous God. *Surrender to me anything that takes precedence in your life:* your love of money, your need to be appreciated and recognized, and your need to fit in. I want your strengths, spiritual gifts, values, and opportunities—anything that you place above me. Give it all to me. I want all the methods you rely on to numb the pain in your life— alcohol, drugs, nicotine, food, shopping, drama, dangerous stunts, and hoarding. None of it will ever satisfy you like I can. I'll have no other gods above me.

I value your passion for my calling on your life. But my dear one, this is my work. *Surrender to me your lifetime dream and your need to feel significant, to make a difference in this world, to matter, to be heard.* I'll be faithful to complete my work, and equally important, I'll be faithful to complete my work in you in my miraculous way and with my timing.

Do you now understand that what I want is you? Not only the parts you choose to give me; not only the parts you can't seem to *make better*; not only the parts you dislike—but all of you. More than anything, I want you in a loving and intimate relationship with me. I want to grow you into spiritual maturity, into a likeness of me. I want to see your faith increase as you experience me in every aspect of your life. *I'm asking you to surrender to me—all of you—now.*

Will you surrender to me all of you, including your lifetime dream?

Will You?

Your Memory Verse, Romans 12:1, reminds you to place your life before God as a living sacrifice. It reads this way from The Message paraphrase:

So here's what I want you to do, God helping you: Take your everyday, ordinary life—your sleeping, eating, going-to-work, and walking-around life—and place it before God as an offering.

What if Jesus actually has whispered a few good ideas to you in this chapter about what to surrender? What if you really were able to acknowledge your role as a humble steward of all God has asked you to manage on earth? Will you, in preparation for your life mission, move forward in at least one area of surrender? In what way will your prayerful insight about surrender specifically impact your day-to-day living and unique life mission—now?

CERTIFICATE OF SURRENDER (TEENAGER)

The earth is the Lord's, and everything in it. The world and all its people belong to him (Psalm 24:1 NLT).

Pray the following prayer if you're ready to surrender one or more things. Take this step at your own pace, without feeling rushed or pressured into it. This is between Jesus and you only.

I Surrender Now

Dear Jesus,

I've counted the cost of surrendering the things I've indicated as I read your letter. I know full well that you may, indeed, take one or more of these things from me, literally. I understand that if you do, it's my responsibility to trust and obey you on a daily, hourly, and minute-by-minute basis. I know that you're acutely aware of how important these things are to me. I love you unconditionally as my Almighty Lord.

In your holy name, I surrender to you these things. Amen.

Signature: _____ Date: _____

Continue praying this prayer if you're ready to surrender everything:

Jesus, I'm content with whatever you choose to give to me or take from me, whether you decide to bless me anymore or not. Everything I have belongs to you, so I leave it all in your hands. Give me the grace to never stop loving you, even if I...

- Lose everything, family and friends included

- Am dirt poor

- Become terminally ill

- Will never be considered a success

- Will never see my dreams come true

- Will never feel like I'm making a profound difference in the world

I freely empty myself of everything except you, so I can be filled by you. I surrender to you all of me, including my lifetime dream.

Your Initials: _____

Memory Verse Chart
Appendix A
Chapters 5-10

Meditate frequently on these Scriptures, letting them remind you to pray for your teenager and yourself. In fact, storm the heavens with prayer, and ask others to pray for your conversations with your teenager. Expect God to reveal fresh insights. Don't forget to point out this chart to your teenager!

Chapter 5: Understanding Your Spiritual Gifts, Best Qualities, and Finest Values

God has given each of you a gift from his great variety of spiritual gifts. Use them well to serve one another (1 Peter 4:10 NLT).

Chapter 6: Rethinking My Motives, Relationships, and Use of Time

People may be pure in their own eyes, but the Lord examines their motives (Proverbs 16:2 NLT).

Chapter 7: Knowing Your Strengths, Weaknesses, Opportunities, and Threats

And I am certain that God, who began the good work within you, will continue his work until it is finally finished on the day when Christ Jesus returns (Philippians 1:6 NLT).

Chapter 8: Praying for Courage, Perseverance, and Miracles

"This is my command—be strong and courageous! Do not be afraid or discouraged. For the Lord your God is with you wherever you go" (Joshua 1:9 NLT).

Chapter 9: Writing Your Lifetime Dream Statement

Many are the plans in a human heart, but it is the Lord's purpose that prevails (Proverbs 19:21 TNIV).

Chapter 10: Surrendering All to Jesus

So here's what I want you to do, God helping you: Take your everyday, ordinary life—your sleeping, eating, going-to-work, and walking-around life—and place it before God as an offering (Romans 12:1 The Message).

Improving Your Conversation Skills
Appendix B

Skill #1: Invite the Holy Spirit.

- Establish a partnership between the Holy Spirit, your teenager, and you.

- Proceed in an atmosphere of trust.

Skill #2: Listen actively.

- Listen reflectively.

- Echo what you hear.

Skill #3: Use the silence; don't fill it.

- Allow your teenager some time to process information.

- Realize that silence may be a self-defense mechanism.

Skill #4: Mind the gap between the spoken and unspoken.

- Pay attention to positive clues (such as enthusiasm, a smile).

- Pay attention to negative clues (such as stubbornness, crossed arms).

Skill #5: Initiate questions.

- Ask questions that clarify a comment.

- Ask questions that suggest a world of possibilities.

Skill #6: Use a simile to get a word picture.

- Ask your teenager to give you a word picture using a simile.

- Give your teenager a word picture using a simile.

Skill #7: Get to the heart of the matter.

- Acknowledge your teenager's emotions.

- Ask a heart question.

Skill #8: Navigate change.

- *Look Out:* Recognize that change is often difficult.

- *Look In:* Replace the negative with the positive.

- *Look Up:* Celebrate victories.

Skill #9: Nudge to move forward.

- Ask action-oriented questions.

- Strategize next steps to take.

Skill #10: Conclude with intentionality.

- Ask your teenager to summarize insights.

- Challenge your teenager and yourself to the memory work.

- Affirm with a positive statement about who your teenager is in Christ.

- Close with a brief, personalized prayer.

How to Make a Commiment to Jesus
Appendix C

If you think you're ready to make a faith commitment to Jesus, here are a few key biblical truths that can help you make your decision:

- **Romans 3:23**   All have sinned; we all fall short.

- **Romans 6:23**   Heaven is a free gift.

- **Romans 5:8**   Jesus, who loves you, has already paid the penalty for your sins by dying on the cross.

- **Romans 10:9-10**   If you confess that Jesus is Lord, and if you believe that God raised Jesus from the dead, you will be saved.

If you're ready, here's a simple prayer you can say:

> *Jesus, I believe that you died for me and that God raised you from the dead. Please forgive my sins. You are my Savior. You are my only hope. I want to follow your will for my life.*

If you prayed that prayer in faith, please let someone know about your decision, so he or she can encourage you to walk out God's grace-filled, purposeful plan for your life.

If you decided not to say a prayer of confession, I urge you to mark this page and to keep seeking truth with an open heart and mind. And don't be shy about asking to talk with a church leader or Christian friend.

How to Cooperate With God
Regarding Your Life Purpose
Appendix D

(Quick-View Reference List of Objectives for Chapters 5-10)

CHAPTER 5: If I understand my spiritual gifts, best qualities, and finest values, I'll see undeniable evidence regarding the specific life work God has assigned me.

CHAPTER 6: If I rethink my motives, relationships, and use of time, I'm better prepared to answer God's call on my life.

CHAPTER 7: If I know myself well—my strengths, weaknesses, opportunities, and threats—God's "This I Must Do" purpose for my life will become clearer and more doable.

CHAPTER 8: If I pray for courage, perseverance, and miracles to help me accomplish my life mission, I'll receive those gifts from God.

CHAPTER 9: If I accept the unique life purpose that God designed specifically for me, I'll have a bold, passionate lifetime dream that far exceeds my highest hopes.

CHAPTER 10: If I surrender my life to Jesus, acknowledging my role as a humble steward of all I've been asked to manage on earth, God will be glorified and I'll be blessed.

How to Contact the Author

To learn more about Katie Brazelton, Ph.D., M.Div., M.A., bestselling author, Life Purpose Coach®, and founder of Life Purpose Coaching Centers International® (LPCCI), and her dream of opening 200 Life Purpose Coaching Centers worldwide, contact her at...

Life Purpose Coaching Centers Intl
P.O. Box 80550-0550
Rancho Santa Margarita, CA 92688
Info@LifePurposeCoachingCenters.com
www.LifePurposeCoachingCenters.com

To invite Katie to give a life-changing, keynote speech (with her special touch of humor) to your organization, contact Ambassador Speakers Bureau in Tennessee at (615) 370-4700 or Naomi@AmbassadorSpeakers.com.

Katie has been a featured guest for radio and television broadcasts, such as *Midday Connection* and *100 Huntley Street*. She's written more than 60 articles for publications such as *Alive!* and *Extraordinary Women*. She's been honored to meet with Mother Teresa in India and other Nobel laureates around the world. She's been invited to speak at such venues as Focus on the Family and the American Association of Christian Counselors' World Conferences.

Currently, Katie is a professor at Rockbridge Seminary, and she served previously as a licensed minister at the purpose driven Saddleback Church in California. Her coach training organization, LPCCI, which is accredited by the International Coach Federation and the International Association of Continuing Education Training, teaches online and on-site, coed, coach training classes. Katie has two adult children, a daughter-in-law and son-in-law, and two precious grandsons. Check out Katie's other purpose series books, DVD, and CD!

The Way I'm Wired: Discovering Who God Made ME to Be

(DVD Youth Curriculum: UPC 646847-16782-9)
simplyyouthministry.com

The Way I'm Wired: Discovering Who God Made ME to Be

(paperback devotional: ISBN 978-0-764-44704-4)
simplyyouthministry.com

- *Pathway to Purpose for Women* (paperback: ISBN 978-0-310-29249-4)

- *Pathway to Purpose for Women* (audio CD: ISBN 978-0-310-26505-4)

- *Pathway to Purpose for Women* (audio download: ISBN 978-0-310-26857-4)

- *Praying for Purpose for Women* (paperback: ISBN 978-0-310-29284-5)

- *Conversations on Purpose for Women** (spiral-bound: ISBN 978-0-310-25650-2)
  (*A few charts in this book were significantly revised and adapted for use in the Wired series.)

- *Character Makeover* (paperback: ISBN 978-0-310-25653-3)

- *Live Big* (paperback: ISBN 978-1-4391-356-0)